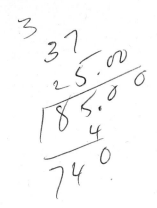

MANY SOVEREIGN

*A case for strengthening state
government—an insider's account*

STATES

by DAN W. LUFKIN

*The former Commissioner of
Environmental Protection of Connecticut
and one of America's leading businessmen
looks at the changing role of the states
in the era of the New Federalism* ·

David McKay Company, Inc.

NEW YORK

Library of Congress Cataloging in Publication Data

Lufkin, Dan W   1931–
    Many sovereign states.

    Includes bibliographical references and index.
        1. State governments.   2. Environmental policy—
Connecticut.   I. Title.
JK2408.L83   353.9   74–25723
ISBN 0–679–50538–5

Preface

by Peter F. Drucker

For forty years, ever since early New Deal days, the "experts" have declared state government to be either dead or dying. The States are "obsolete"; they are reactionary and incapable of effective action, let alone of innovation; they are hopelessly corrupt—these were the standard judgments which by now have become commonplace in practically every American classroom. At the very least, theorists suggested that the "historical accidents" of our fifty states be replaced by a small number of rational "regions." Or, the favorite proposal of the Kennedy years, the "do-nothing" state should be rendered innocuous through an "activist," "dynamic" and "liberal" partnership between the federal government and the big cities.

Yet the patient has refused to die. Indeed, during the last twenty years—at the very time when "expert" after "expert" declared the states dead—he has undergone a renaissance. It would not be too much of an exaggeration to say that the most important and most lasting development in American constitutional and political structure of the last twenty years has been the resurgence of state government.

For twenty years, from the early years of the Depression through the Korean War, federal revenues and federal expenditures grew phenomenally, and the big cities also experienced a sizable growth in expenditures and revenues. Since the Korean War the share of federal government expenditure in the American Gross National Product has actually declined. But during the same period the revenues and expenditures of the states have increased dramatically—to the point where their total budgets bid fair to rival the federal budget, especially if defense is excluded. Equally startling has been the growth in employment. Even small states are now very large employers, especially of educated people—engineers, accountants, health scientists and so on.

But perhaps more important than this economic shift has been the quantitative change in the position of the state government in American political life. For the first time in forty years, state governors are again becoming important national figures in their own right—a Rockefeller, a Reagan, a Romney, or a George Wallace. Following the Supreme Court decision of *Baker v. Carr,* "one man, one vote," state legislatures have again become capable of performance and action—though a great deal remains to be done. In one state at least, California, an imaginative state political leader, Jesse Unruh, used the Supreme Court decision to create a state legislature which is better organized, better disciplined and far more capable of performance than either the U.S. House of Representatives or the U.S. Senate.

Above all, we are rapidly discovering that the states, far from being "obsolete" are now more important than they have been since the early days of the Republic. They are more important, both in the traditional roles and in new roles.

They are, first, again becoming capable of policy innovation—the most important of their traditional roles. In respect to the environment, the pioneering work, both in terms of public awareness and in terms of legislation, was done at a state level in the Northeast and along the Pacific Coast. A state commissioner of insurance, Walter Dennenberg of Pennsylvania, has probably done more for consumer protection and with more lasting results than such much more widely publicized figures as Ralph Nader on the national scene—and Dennenberg did it in the seemingly traditional and hidebound field of insurance regulation. While the federal government, in the area of urban transportation, has so far done little but spend money, Pennsylvania, in and around Philadelphia, has actually led in the effort to improve mass transit. Former Governor Reagan's attempt to force a rational budget process on the legislature, through a constitutional ceiling on state expenditures, was defeated at the polls in 1973; but there is little doubt that this or some similar plan will have to be adopted if the control of public expenditures is to return to elected representatives of the people. Similarly, former Governor Rockefeller's attempt to bring order to the chaotic welfare situation, while not the final answer, is an encouraging sign that such complex problems may have feasible solutions. And so on.

At the same time, however, the state government is emerging in a new role: as the instrument through which national—and possibly also international—policy can alone become effective. This is particularly true in such major areas as the environment, energy, and land-use planning—areas in which there are "trade-offs," that is, areas in which a gain always has to be paid for; areas in which costs need to be weighed against benefits; areas in which one good, e.g., jobs, needs to be balanced against another good, e.g., clean water; areas in which one group will have to make sacrifices for the sake of another group or of the community. These "trade-offs" can best be made on the local level, since conditions differ from area to area and only the intimate knowledge of the local conditions, which is available at the state level, can find the balance which is fair, appropriate and equitable in a given situation.

These "trade-off" decisions must be based on local consensus to be effective. If they are not, as the experience with ambitious national programs during the last decade has amply shown, the local community will succeed in stymieing and sabotaging even the most badly needed and most soundly conceived "big program." No one lives in the "big picture." It is pure abstraction. There is no such thing as "the environment." There are the conditions at a given coastline, in a given industrial valley or along the banks of a specific polluted river. Unless the action taken fits the coastline and the people who live along it, the industrial valley and people whose livelihood depends on the jobs therein, and the individual stream with all the riparian inhabitants and interests, nothing will be done. The states alone can translate big, badly needed national and international policies into truly effective action.

The states thus emerge in the new role as the effective *partners* in national, and even international, policy. They are not just "organs," which carry out the orders from the center. They have to be partners which take national goals and turn them into effective and appropriate action on the state and community levels.

Finally, we increasingly realize that state action or state inaction are not just "local" matters which can safely be relegated to the back pages of the local newspapers. The states are interdependent to an extent our forefathers could not have foreseen. The "welfare mess" of the big northern cities, for instance, is to a considerable extent the result of the lack of attention to poverty, welfare, and education in the states of the Deep South. State policies, therefore, need to be framed by people who can think nationally—and increasingly internationally; who can relate what seem to be purely local problems to a much bigger world and who can give true leadership in the making of policy. And this too endows the states and their governments with new importance and impact.

There is still a great deal badly wrong with many, if not with all, state governments. Corruption is still a "way of life" in many state houses—though at least corrupt state politicians now find themselves increasingly indicted and convicted—in Maryland, in New Jersey, in Illinois, and in Texas. Even in many important states, state government is almost totally disorganized and parcelled out among competing political machines and pressure groups. There are still states—and populous ones, such as Alabama—in which the governor is paid less than the federal government pays an apprentice mailman. State legislatures, only too often, serve no other purpose than to give aspiring young lawyers access to lobbying fees and lobbying clients.

But perhaps the greatest weakness of state government is that far too few people have yet realized its resurgence, its importance and the opportunities it offers for effective public service. This country does not lack young successful men, whether in business or in the professions, who hanker for the opportunity to give effective service and to make a contribution. But the young man who recognizes that the government of his own state may well be the place where he can serve best and make the most telling contribution the fastest is still a very rare exception.

One of these exceptions is Dan Lufkin. Having built, in a few years of very hard work, one of the country's leading investment banks, he decided—in the best American tradition—to dedicate some years of his life to the public service. He then bid for and secured the thorniest, most difficult and "hottest" seat in the American politics of the early seventies: appointment as the first Commissioner of Environmental Protection in an industrial state, Connecticut. His performance in this difficult assignment was outstanding. His ability to balance conflicting interests and to do full justice to the environment and yet retain support and understanding not only set a standard that will be hard to match. It also shows that the environmental job, however difficult, can be done, and how it has to be approached.

But Dan Lufkin's most enduring contribution and his most important one is probably this present book. It is not

the book of a "political scientist" or a "professional politician." It is the book of a sensitive, intelligent, imaginative
human being—a record of personal frustration and problems, but also of accomplishment and public service. It
does not discuss state government in the abstract. Yet it
projects a clearly thought through, clearly articulated picture of the political and governmental process at the state
level—of people, forces, interests, needs and problems, and
above all, of opportunity. *Many Sovereign States* will not
only help many citizens to understand how state government
in general, and their state government in particular, work
—and why it is important for them to take an interest in its
working. It will, also, I hope, inspire a good many others
to see in state government a unique, challenging, and re-
warding opportunity for service.

Claremont, California

Contents

MANY SOVEREIGN STATES

CHAPTER 1

The Lively Graveyard

★

I am not a professional politician, a career bureaucrat, an historian or a lifelong student of comparative government. In the spirit of so many of my contemporaries in post World War II America, I went to Yale, attended Harvard Business School, gained experience working for someone else and then, in company with good friends and classmates, at age twenty-eight, I took the long chance of starting my own business in the financial services, asset management field. In late 1959, Donaldson, Lufkin & Jenrette, Inc. was born and took up residence on Wall Street.

Our business prospered. At first, it absorbed all our energies. There was a new challenge, a new risk, a new adventure, and always the delight of seeing our work rewarded in a competitive environment. Our success depended on the confidence which others were willing to place in our financial judgment and our business decisions. As asset managers, we opened up new frontiers of investment growth, initially specializing in smaller companies for the institutional market which were generally overlooked or viewed with skepticism by the Wall Street establishment of the late 50s and early 60s.

Our business gradually broadened beyond this initial specialty, and in the course of ten years, our services multiplied into a full, broad-based investment banking concern and our original investment grew beyond our fondest hopes. We had been working so hard in such a challenging and changing environment that in the process we had not thought out our own lives much beyond the next annual report, which, as far as I could tell, put us right in step with virtually all our contemporaries who hadn't either.

Somewhere along in the late 60s, I realized that the bright young business school graduates, the industry specialists, the professionals were proving themselves equal to the job of maintaining and even improving on what we had begun. After the initial shock, I looked at the brighter side. I found that I did not have to remain tied to the sunless canyons of the city, but rather had time to commute an hour or so a day. And so I searched the area surrounding New York City for a working farm community, farming having been a lifelong love of mine.

I drew a figurative circle with its center in Central Park and then investigated those areas of New Jersey, New York, and Connecticut which lay within its radius. I was amazed by what I found. The entire character of the land changed completely as I followed the industrial belt of New Jersey into the quiet, rolling landscape of Connecticut.

In the one state, there seemed to be unrelieved industry and the environmental blight that went with it. Highways and railroad sidings. Palls of noxious smoke from chemical plants and oil refineries. Slag heaps, auto graveyards, and stretches of polluted waterways. In Connecticut, there were mill towns and ancient brick factories, yes, but interspersed with these were the hills, farms, rural villages, and suburbs that form the gentle fabric of Connecticut and give it its unique character and charm.

And so, my wife, Elise, and I chose Connecticut as a place to farm and to raise our children. The "important" business could be done in the city only an hour or so away. The dream of a working farm could be realized in the woods and meadows of Upper Fairfield County, still largely rural. There was a world of work and a world of delight.

Occasionally I commuted to the city by helicopter. Each day's journey was a new and unpleasant lesson in urban sprawl and decay, pollution, the transportation crisis, and the chaos of unplanned, unordered land use. From the air, New York City, its suburbs, and its Connecticut exurbs provided a living textbook of environmental, economic, social and political science. Almost in spite of myself, I began to absorb the lessons of each unfolding chapter of this troubled text. I had been an investment banker and a farmer. After I moved to Connecticut, I became something else as well—an angry critic of environmental degradation in all of its varied manifestations.

Some mornings as we flew beyond the valleys of my home, the entire area was obscured by the squalid veil of an air inversion system. Often Manhattan Island lay inert beneath a covering of nauseous green smog which knew no state boundaries. As we swept slowly overhead, I could see a rainbow of colored effluents pouring into rivers, lakes, and Long Island Sound. Smokestacks poured out thick black plumes. On the scores of highways gouged out of thousands of acres of good Connecticut farmland, a million commuters crept towards work in the film of their own exhausts.

Cutting Connecticut in half was an ugly strip of freeways, factory towns, railheads, monotonous residential developments, and shopping centers. It wound its way north from Stamford through Hartford on up to Enfield and the borders of Massachusetts. It was almost as if New York were being squeezed into Connecticut from a grease gun. And there were unmistakable signs that this swath of industry and urbanization was increasing each day—unplanned and uncompromising. Here, the countryside was being denuded to make way for a new spur of highway.

There, as far as the eye could see, a power line was being hacked through a wooded hillside. And everywhere the bulldozers were scraping off the ancient, delicate ground cover to make way for a new development or industrial park.

Despite my personal history and my strong belief in an economic system based on industrial growth and development, I could not help but be deeply disturbed by these daily reminders of the advancing abuses of our land, our air, and our water. I could not help but feel a profound sadness for the cheated men and women, who were exchanging their inheritance of countryside for smog, traffic, and crowded urban habitation, who were—often unknowingly—sacrificing their chance for a humane quality of life. Flying over the illogical cities, I understood the smoldering rage of those trapped in totally "denatured" environments.

As the unspoiled beauty of my own farm became more precious to me, I began to wonder how long it could remain immune from assault. And I began to ask myself how many others like me, who owned a farm or a home, or swam in a lake, or enjoyed a picnic in a park or forest, were even now in the process of losing this life to new highways, to the fumes of new factories, or to the insensitivity of land use, based only on a single, narrow economic criterion.

I began to question the people who should know the answers. The selectmen, the mayors, the state legislators. Where were these decisions being made? Was there any state or regional planning? Weren't federal and state laws being broken by the polluters and was there no means of enforcing these laws? Did Connecticut's need for tax revenues mean that industry was welcome everywhere? Did the residents of Connecticut's 169 towns and cities have any means of expressing their own preferences for a way of life? Could the utilities simply commandeer the land for their power lines and generating stations whenever *their* experts said that more energy was needed? Were there any controls at all on industrial growth? Any balance? Should there be? And whose decision was it anyway? The more difficult it was to find answers to these questions, the less satisfied I was with my role as a transient between home and job, and the more I found myself a concerned and angry citizen of my state.

Inevitably, the transformation became complete. No longer a commuter, I was now a resident of Connecticut—tax paying, voting, and, in a special and singular way, caring.

There is a saying that every American has two hometowns, his own and San Francisco. When I was a boy growing up in New York, Connecticut was always a second home to me. It was, really, the only state I knew. For, if I called myself a New Yorker, it meant that I belonged to the city. Albany, Syracuse, and Schenectady were as foreign to my experience as Rome, Paris, and Vienna.

But Connecticut, as a state, became imprinted early on my consciousness. First, when my parents took me with them while visiting friends in southwestern Connecticut, in Fairfield County. Later, I went to school in the northwest corner of the state and began to savor its native delights more deeply. At Hotchkiss, I remember vividly the hockey games played on the black ice of Long Pond and the skating drills on the lake atop Mt. Riga with wonderful old Tom Hall. After a long winter afternoon on the ice, the winter majesty of virgin Mt. Riga is impossible to forget.

I have lasting memories of the rocks at Guilford and the spit of land that runs to the breakwater of New Haven Harbor, where I did some of my earliest (and most successful) duck hunting. Vividly, I can still recall fishing the Housatonic River in the early spring in the fly-fishing stretch below Cornwall Bridge and the joy of another

Connecticut spring awakening on the shores of that gorgeous river.

One summer, I worked for the Gulf Oil Corporation at its terminal in South Norwalk. It was in that summer that I got to know with some intimacy the small mill towns which are so much a part of the unique fabric of Connecticut; towns built on the riverways whose waters were once clear and filled with fish, and now are brown, sluggish paths of municipal and industrial waste.

Yet, until I became a resident of Connecticut, it remained only a state of mind—a montage of pleasant images and emotions, but in no sense a place to which I belonged and certainly not one about which I had any urgent feeling of responsibility. That feeling was born at 3,000 feet, chopping through the smog toward New York City and a job that increasingly seemed less important than the challenge of trying to see what could be done to help.

Theorizing at 3,000 feet is one thing. Asking questions of neighbors, town officials, and local representatives is another. How does one ordinary citizen find an attaching point to a state so that he can make himself an instrument of change? "Give me a place to stand," said Archimedes, "and I will move the earth." In some ways, that challenge seemed easier than setting in place a lever to move one small state.

In Connecticut, the tradition of volunteerism is old and strong. There are literally hundreds of citizens' organizations concerned with everything from the preservation of the osprey to the legislative approval of an official state song. What was lacking, it seemed to me, was an organization which would support and encourage informed voluntary action by providing resources for planning, research, and funding, on a small scale, demonstration programs in one or two areas.

A small group of us, led by Rita Bowlby and Tina

Harrower and drawing on a wide range of volunteer help across the state, decided that they key word was action and that the time was now. And so in late 1969 Connecticut Action Now was born. We opened an office in New Haven and constructed an agenda that centered on the environment, both natural and unnatural—the living countryside as well as the dying urban ghetto.

Suddenly the problems I had been observing from a distance became very close, very personal, and very real. A family in New Haven was being dispossessed. A crisis intervention center in Hartford was being closed. A plating plant in Bristol was violating water quality standards. The problems overloaded the capacities of our small staff, and their total solutions seemed impossible to attain through merely voluntary action. The individual citizen was certainly a vital element in the equation of problem solving. But without adequate resources, planning, and programs, even the most enlightened zeal was not enough. And unless the official machinery of government was involved, solutions became recommendations, recommendations were amended, and because they were unofficial and could not be enforced, they were finally ignored.

Gradually, Connecticut Action Now devoted more of its limited resources to the natural environment in the cities and suburbs. The degradation of Connecticut's land, water, and air was a growing concern of every citizen. New federal regulations were placing increased responsibilities on state government. Yet both the resources and the will for compliance and enforcement seemed lacking in the diffuse, sometimes partisan and always overlapping authorities charged with the protection of Connecticut's quality of life.

So Connecticut Action Now became an environmental gadfly, urging citizens to a more aggressive defense of the state's natural resources and presenting Connecticut's elected officials with the hard data necessary to underwrite

the economic risk of passing tougher environmental protection laws.

What was even more significant was the way in which
general principles quickly were narrowed down to particular cases. It was not the "big issue" of water pollution we
grappled with, but the discharge of a specific effluent from
a particular point source along the Pequabuck River. Not
just the "theoretical" issue of preserving tidal wetlands
concerned us but the filling in of a particular wetland by a
specific corporation in violation of a very real piece of
legislation.

I was amazed to see how responsive the machinery of
state government could be to the pressure from informed
and concerned citizens. I discovered that state government
was not just "machinery" disinterestedly cranking out
legislation. The machinery was people, men and women
who lived in the small towns and cities, who cared about
the state because it was their home. They gave serious
consideration to their actions because they and their
children would have to live with them long after their
terms of office had ended.

Within months of the establishment of Connecticut
Action Now, I found myself discussing with Stanley Pac,
then co-chairman of the legislature's Environment Committee, the need for pulling together all the diverse
environmental authorities of the state into a single department or agency which would have broad powers of
coordination, regulation, and enforcement.

Now, it is one thing to determine that something must
be done about a problem and quite another to muster both
the courage and the votes to do it. I had been warned
about the painful slowness of the state bureaucracy, the
logrolling and back-scratching, the "show me" skepticism with which the country folk who had traditionally
dominated state legislatures approached anything that

threatened to change what was familiar and accepted, particularly in the area of environmental control.

Add to this the real concern that the legislature would be strongly influenced by the traditional health, agricultural, and fish and game bureaucracies, who had divided among themselves the responsibility for environmental protection.

We were wrong. Simply stated, we were wrong. Not only did we underestimate the power of environmental protection as an idea whose time had come, but we misjudged badly the quality of legislative leadership—such men as state senators Stanley Pac, George Gunther, and Roger Eddy—and the skill with which it was able to read the will of the electorate. The people of Connecticut were as fed up as the environmental activists with the ineffective patchwork of agencies and commissions which had been responsible for cleaning the air and water and preserving the character of the land. They were angry with the total inability of the bureaucracy to pursue the chronic violators of the law and to force them to stop their polluting. While Connecticut Action Now had been collecting data and researching the pending environmental legislation, the people of the state had been busy. They had telephoned their representatives, had written angry letters, had attended town meetings and state hearings, and had expressed unmistakably their insistence that something positive must be done.

The leadership of the Environmental Committee overrode our caution. They had sized up the sentiment of both houses on both sides of the aisle. Because they had done their homework, they were able to produce an acceptable bill that would mandate a drastic reorganization of state government.

In many ways, it was one of the most all-inclusive environmental acts that any state legislature could be asked to approve, or, in fact, ever has been approved. It was a pioneer bill, and there were holes in it and administrative weaknesses and some overlap. But it worked and it passed. And now, the leadership said, it would be up to everyone who had been pleading for the bill to make it a success.

The circumstances and timing of the passage of Connecticut's Environmental Protection Act provided a textbook case in the working of our federal system and its interrelationship with the states. In the absence of national policy, the states, over a period of years, had developed a haphazard method of coping with problems whose seriousness was apparent, but whose solution involved potential conflicts and confrontations between the most powerful interest groups within and among the states.

Environmental pollution is the product of the same system which has brought us our material abundance and national prosperity. Industry, agriculture, and the machines and materials which comprise our individual comfort and convenience—automobiles, air conditioners, detergents, plastics—produce the wastes that poison our air, land, and water. Growth, the keystone of our economic progress, creates an insatiable demand for goods and services which not only use up finite raw materials but inevitably change the balance of our ecosystem.

For many years the ecosystem was defended by a few evangelistic prophets—people like Barry Commoner and Ian McHarg nationally and Bill Niering, biologist at Connecticut College, and Russ Brenneman, a Hartford lawyer. Eventually, they alarmed enough citizens to produce the earliest federal and state environmental legislation. But even when clean air and water regulations were put on the books, enforcement was less than halfhearted. Opposition in the name of prosperity and progress was generally too powerful to overcome, and the committee mechanics of enforcement dictated conflict. The Clean Air

Commission in Connecticut is a case in point. A committee representing directly conflicting interests, it watered down or buried virtually all meaningful enforcement procedures to come before it. Were it not for the courageous stands of a few of its members, led by Dr. Rita Kaunitz, who lives in Westport, the public might still be misled about the "progress" towards clean air in the early 70s. Beyond such conflict, citizen boards, like the clean air committee, tried to give part-time direction and supervision to state bodies whose basic responsibilities and interests were elsewhere, and whose resources were already overtaxed.

The problems of enforcing environmental regulation were further complicated by the fact that the various branches of state government are evaluated largely on the basis of their economic performance. No matter how idealistic or humane a governor may be, most citizens judge him by the way he has protected their pocketbooks and guarded the treasury of the state. (Governors who propose state income taxes habitually find themselves looking for a new job after the next election.) Because the states had failed to provide effective legislation to protect their natural resources and to clean up the damage done to their environment, concerned citizens turned to the federal Congress for action. As a result, national standards were mandated and major funds voted to give the states the leverage needed either to initiate or raise their standards and finance the requirements imposed by the new laws.

A major advantage of national environmental standards is that they bring every state up to a minimum acceptable level. If, for example, Connecticut passes tough air quality standards and Massachusetts does not, Connecticut industry is tempted to fold up business and move to Massachusetts, or to another state where large antipollution investments are not mandatory. Federal regulations which place burdens equally on all states make it far more likely that industry will comply rather than try to escape. Now, with everyone conforming to federal standards, there is no escape—no place to hide.

At the time of the legislative debate over Connecticut's Environmental Protection Act, the spring of 1971, the Federal Air Quality Act had just come into being. Under it, there would be no place to hide for Connecticut's violators of air quality standards. But the development of a state program to meet these exacting federal standards would require far more expertise, professionalism, and objectivity than had previously been manifested by the old committee structure. While policy would be federal, enforcement would clearly be state responsibility, and the state had to be in a position to exercise this responsibility or lose it.

Other federal legislation in water pollution would impose even greater burdens on the many separate state commissions exercising partial and overlapping jurisdictions in these environmental fields. With a national Environmental Protection Agency organized to set policy and supervise the complete gamut of environmental programs, the pressure was on the states to create a mechanism which could deal with the federal bureaucracy on its own terms, speak its language, and take advantage of the federal grants-in-aid soon to become available to the states for the implementation and coordination of their programs.

Federal policy-making places a sharp burden on the states to be effective or lose control of their own destinies. When Congress reacts to the public outrage over pollution, great pressure is placed on the executive branch. It must get organized, get moving, show results or lose the political high ground that the legislation was designed to capture. Passage of federal law does not necessarily mean that local implementation is going to take place. And the bureaucracy in Washington, under the gun of Congress and the President to get the job done, is nevertheless reluctant to work through the states, which it considers inefficient, foot-dragging, lacking in manpower and brain power, and subject to intense local pressure to delay performance or not to perform at all.

For years, these were among the most persuasive arguments that led to the concentration of power in Washington, with federal agencies not only setting policy but actually administering their own programs through regional and local offices. Theoretically, such direct control may seem more effective than reliance on the state. But, in practice, such total control has proved to be not only unresponsive but unworkable.

The federal bureaucracies, too, are subject to the pressures of a broad and often conflicting set of constituencies. They must please the Executive branch, deal with the Office of Management and Budget, work in cooperation with governors and mayors, satisfy the demands of a variety of committees on the Hill, many times led by unrepresentative chairmen, and then pass on their decisions to the federal presence which is trying to cope with local problems. There are more than sixteen thousand point sources of air pollution in Connecticut. Multiply these by the millions discharging emissions into the skies of America, and the magnitude of the problem of enforcement and control becomes apparent when addressed on the federal level.

No federal agency can stretch its resources of manpower and money to assure the investigation, analysis, enforcement, and monitoring of every source of pollution in every state. That should be a job for the people who have the greatest stake in pure air or clean water for Connecticut, New York, or Minnesota—the people who live there. The federal government can propose, but only the state officials, on the spot and responsible to the voters, can effectively dispose. There are too many hiding places in the federal bureaucracy. But, on the local level, there is no place to hide. The lake or river must be cleaned or some bureaucrat's neighbors are going to toss him out of office, see that he is roasted in the press, or pay a forceful and well-publicized visit to his agency.

Traveling to Washington is obviously impractical every time there is a complaint; even finding the right person or organization to complain to can frustrate the most ardent activist. Writing to a Congressman is fine because he's a neighbor, too. But he's a neighbor who now lives in Washington, and who has no line authority in his state. Ultimately, the responsibility is going to come right back to that arm of local government which is nearest to the offending smokestack discharging SO_2 and particulates over Bridgeport.

In June of 1971, Connecticut passed Public Act 872 creating a single environmental department out of a smorgasbord of eighteen different commissions, boards, committees, and agencies. Pressure of pending federal environmental legislation, and local demand from the voters, squeezed the disparate and disorganized environmental overseers into a unified establishment with broad powers. Once down on paper, it had three months' lead time to pull itself into shape and begin to function.

Bill Ruckelshaus, who was the first, and very effective, Federal Environmental Protection Administrator, has said that getting EPA set up and functioning was like running the hundred-yard dash while performing an appendectomy. Although I had never performed an appendectomy, even while standing still, he asked me, shortly after he was appointed, to come to Washington as his number-two man. I declined this offer; but when Governor Thomas J. Meskill asked me to organize and head up Connecticut's first Department of Environmental Protection, I accepted. Soon I, too, found that within the limited confines of the state, there is no place to hide.

I took the state job, rather than the federal job, for many reasons. It was "my" state, and almost by definition of state citizenship, its problems were my problems. Equally important, I had become increasingly frustrated by the distance and impersonality of federal authority. Somehow, I felt, the states had to become more sensitive, responsible mechanisms of change if they were to play the important role tentatively designed for them under the "New Federalism."

The national government had too many priorities to deal with before it could be bothered with the improvement of the quality of life in Connecticut. For the state government, that clearly should be the *only* item on its agenda. I was determined to do what I could to help, both Connecticut and the system.

When the announcement of my appointment was made by the governor, the first call I received was from a noted New York industrialist who had shuttled in and out of high places in the federal establishment during the administrations of four Presidents.

"My God, Dan," he said, "if you had government service in mind, why didn't you tell me? I'm sure we could have gotten you whatever you wanted.

"But state service?" He paused and took a deep breath. "It's a graveyard, Dan. A graveyard."

During two years in state government, I found that graveyard to be a most lively and challenging place. Far from being dead, the state is a center of action and responsibility. Instead of a collection of dull and lifeless ghosts, I found an assortment of talented and committed men and women at all levels of state government.

During the time I served as commissioner of Environmental Protection, I asked myself: Why is state government underrated and maligned? Why has the federal government superseded the states in power, responsibility, and prestige? What role do the states have in the solution of America's great social, economic, and political problems? What needs to be done to restore the states to a position of full partnership with the federal government in creating a better life for the American people? This book is my answer.

To the legions of devoted, but unsung, inhabitants of that most lively graveyard—the thousands of state and local officials, legislators and civil servants—I dedicate the results of my two-year attempt to think through the role of the states in America's future. Thanks largely to them, I am optimistic enough to believe that the troubled states will once again become the "dynamic states"—where the process of giving shape and direction to America's third century will be centered and where there is—thank heavens—no place to hide.

CHAPTER 2

A Smattering of History— and a New Definition of States' Rights

★

If the states had not existed before the nation, they would inevitably have been invented. This continent is too large and varied, its inhabitants are too diverse, to permit a completely homogenized nationhood. While today there may seem to be little apparent reason for the shape of California, the division between North and South Dakota, or the very existence of Rhode Island, the states are an essential fact of American life. Not only do they diversify the color scheme of the map but they scale down comfortably our thinking about the huge land mass that is our national home.

Because we are a country of strangers, very few of us have strong ties to the totality of the American experience, either historically or geographically. Most of our ancestors came from the nation states of Europe. Wherever they settled in America, they gave a distinctive character to their new homes and strongly identified with their new national and cultural heritage.

When I was in the Marines, I remember that the first and most basic question we asked one another was "Where are you from?" The answer was never a grand "I am an American," but an instant identification with a particular state. And when a newfound friend answered New York or Georgia or Kansas, we had a strong instinctive sense of what that meant, even though we may never have been there. The accents of the young recruits were varied. Their attitudes and experiences were vastly different as well. Very often long-established stereotypes came to life: the big talker from Texas, the laconic Vermont dairy farmer, the hustler from New York. Hollywood-organized platoons, which fought World War II in every movie theater, were made up of these archetypes of American statehood.

We saw the archetypes come to life, but we also saw new dimensions added to our perceptions of American life. Inevitably, we filed these perceptions in the convenient pigeonholes of states or regions. New York was more than Brooklyn or Manhattan. Mississippi was not all backwardness and bigotry. Farm boys from the Plains States were often more sophisticated than their citified cousins from the industrial East.

The attitudes of these young men toward their states were varied and colorful as well. America, as a whole, was too big to be grasped by them in its entirety. The strongest influences on them were what they had seen and done, or not yet seen and done, in their own hometowns and their own states. Moving to California was a widely shared dream. Leaving the city to ranch in Montana or Colorado or Oregon was another. So was making it big on Wall Street or striking it rich in Texas. And when, at night, in darkened barracks at Quantico or colder tents in Korea, these young men swapped lies about their past or exchanged dreams of their future, we knew instinctively what they meant. We understood what they were thinking and feeling when they talked about the states they called home, or those that some day they intended to call home.

The states are rooted deep in the American consciousness. We can sing "My Country 'Tis of Thee." We can even fight and die for the United States. But the sense of belonging to a piece of that continent labeled Maine or Illinois goes as deep, or deeper. It defines much of what constitutes being an American. It is not only a designation of residence, but the frame of reference within which we comprehend ourselves and our nation.

Almost two hundred years after Connecticut defined itself as a state, the Connecticut Yankee is still a very distinct species, indeed. He adds a special quality to the life of the state, imparting a kind of instant tradition, a ready-to-wear value system to the immigrants from other states who take up residence in Connecticut each day.

There are little old ladies in tennis shoes who live in California, and there are sturdy farm women in Iowa; but it could only have been a Connecticut bluestocking who accosted me in the State Capitol soon after I became Commissioner of Environmental Protection.

"You're a disgrace and a fraud," she said, her cold blue eyes examining me mercilessly.

"You know, sometimes I think you're right," I said, "but what particular disgrace are you referring to?"

"Your cigar," she said. "You preach a healthy environment, but you smoke a cigar."

"Ah, but I don't inhale," I said.

"I don't care about *you*," she snapped, "but you're polluting the air *I* have to breathe."

Somehow, I think the scenario would have been a little different in the capitols of New Jersey or North Dakota (and maybe the cigar would have been, too, since I smoke only Grave's best—and they *do* smell).

Although psychological and emotional identification with the states is still strong, their viability has been sharply discounted in recent years. Great national issues like wars, depressions, and revolutions in values have seemed to require both national solutions and centralized administration.

"States' rights," over the years, became a code word for resistance to national policy and even stubborn refusal to obey national law. There is a considerable body of opinion which holds that the states have long been obsolete—part of the past—and that it would be a total waste of energy to try to drag them into the future.

"No prominent thinkers have defended the states in recent years," [1] says Ira Sharkansky in his book *The Maligned States.* (After reading this charge, I momentarily questioned whether I should continue this book.) Terry Sanford, former governor of North Carolina, quotes a statement from a 1933 article by Luther Gulick: "The American state is finished. I do not predict the states will go but affirm that they have gone." [2]

Reports of the states' demise have been premature. Not only have they broad powers of legislation and taxation, as granted by the Constitution, but under the still-forming doctrine of the "New Federalism," they will have increased duties and responsibilities together with increased resources.

Although some die-hards are still nostalgic for "interposition" and "nullification," it is generally accepted that the federal government has sole responsibility for establishing domestic policy, while the states are the primary vehicle for carrying it out. In fact, the most heated arguments about the workings of the federal system are now directed at the powers of the Executive branch which have proliferated at the expense of the Legislative and Judicial. Dire prophecies have been uttered about the death of Congress and the captivity of the Supreme Court. The states have come of age in the 1970s. In the intricate network of checks and balances, rights and obligations, which characterizes our system of government, the states seem to be achieving new significance as an important, if not yet full, partner of the federal branches.

Certainly, the framers of the Articles of Confederation, which brought the thirteen states together into a loose *federal* system, did not contemplate an eventual withering away of the states in favor of a unitary form of centralized authority. They titled their document "The Articles of Perpetual Union," and they called their new union "The United States of America," placing great emphasis throughout the document on the word *states*.

What these earliest Americans intended was a firm league of friendship for their common defense, the security of their liberties, and their mutual and general welfare. Although the ultimate power was to reside in the states, which had willingly created the union, the final Article of Confederation admonished every state to "abide by the determinations of the United States on all questions which, by this Confederation, are submitted to them."

In the decade between 1777 and 1787, it became increasingly clear that the form of union contemplated by the Articles of Confederation was not workable as a perpetual or self-maintaining political system. As the expression of a theory of government, it was admirable. During the years of the Revolution, when the thirteen states were united against a common enemy, it even proved effective in accomplishing the difficult, though limited, task of winning a war.

After the war, however, the differences, the jealousies, and the competition between the states began to assert themselves until the more serious patriots and political philosophers feared for the safety of their country.

Philosophically, the underlying theme of the Articles of Confederation was a distrust of strong centralized govern-

ment. The radicals, like Samuel Adams, who had pushed
the document through to ratification were those who had
chafed most under the absolute rule of the English king
and Parliament. They believed that a strong central
government would inevitably become the tool of rich
merchants, planters, and other members of the colonial
elite—concerns which certainly have their modern counterparts. They were unwilling to trade the corrupt, authoritarian, and distant regime of George III for a homegrown
variety which might prove to be just as corruptible and
equally authoritarian.

What the leadership of the thirteen states wanted was
strong local government whose diversity of interest would
prevent too much concentration of power and whose
mutuality of purpose—trade, defense, and interstate services—would establish a central mechanism to direct foreign policy, float a navy, run a postal service, make
treaties, and do little else. But practically speaking, the
Articles of Confederation lacked two essential powers
which any federal government needs to survive—the
power to tax, and the means to guarantee that the states
would live up to the nation's treaties with foreign powers.

Before the Declaration of Independence, all plans for
forming a union of the colonies had presupposed as an
inescapable fact of life the ultimate authority of the British
government. Once independence was proclaimed, the
challenge handed the colonial leadership was to find a
substitute for the political authority wielded by Great
Britain. The forces distrustful of centralized authority at
first carried the day. In the proposed confederation, the
national government became the agent of the states which
remained superior to it.

By the time the Constitutional Convention was called,
however, the shakiness of the Confederation had become
apparent, and the conservatives took the offensive. As
proposed by them, and ultimately accepted by the now

weary advocates of state supremacy, the decisive voice of authority was given to the national government. Although all other powers not otherwise defined were retained by the states, the Constitution adopted in 1789 strongly consolidated the ultimate authority in the national capital.

The Articles of Confederation had called for a "perpetual union" among equal powers who delegated out of strength and retained the most significant elements of decision-making for themselves. The Constitution was designed to create "a more perfect union," guaranteeing a broad range of rights to the citizens of the United States, but establishing itself as the final arbiter of national policy. Under the Constitution, the states retained the appearance of power and authority, but there was little doubt that if it came to a showdown, the central government held all the aces.

The Civil War was the most convulsive test of the subordination of states' rights to national policy. The argument was won by those advocating centralized government, and for the next century, the states lay in the shadow of failed secession and thwarted supremacy.

It is interesting to note that when Canada wrote its own federal constitution in 1867, its awareness of the horrors of our Civil War propelled it toward a stronger central government than the Canadians might otherwise have adopted. As a result, the British North America Act is more strongly centrist than most other federal constitutions. The national government has the power to veto the acts of provincial legislatures, and it has exercised this power. Canada's senate, unlike the upper house in the United States, does not provide equal representation for the provinces. In each of the provincial capitals, the lieutenant governors are designated by the national government, and serve in each province as symbols of national power and authority.

Despite the fact that our federal Constitution gives far

more authority to the United States Government than the
Articles of Confederation contemplated, the states have all
of the powers they need to manage affairs within their
borders. In fact, they retain all of the powers it is possible
for any government to have except as they themselves
have delegated these powers to the national government or
have limited their own scope of action through the
provisions of their state constitutions.

The thirteen states which entered into the original
agreement were, at the time, independent and sovereign.
Surrendering specific portions of their sovereignty was not
lightly done. Beyond these specific grants of powers, their
clear intent—as expressed in the Tenth Amendment,
added in 1791—was that "The powers not delegated to the
United States by the Constitution, nor prohibited by it to
the States, are reserved to the States respectively, or to the
people."

Under John Marshall, the Supreme Court tended to
interpret the Constitution as placing the national government irrevocably in a position superior to the states, and
to assert that the supremacy clause of Article 6 meant
exactly that. But by the time Andrew Jackson became
President, the pendulum had swung back to a more
favorable view of states' rights. As President, Jackson told
the Cherokee Indians in 1832 when they petitioned him to
redress certain grievances, "The President of the United
States has no power to protect you against the laws of
Georgia."

From Marshall's death in 1835 to the beginning of the
Civil War, the states' rights theory was ascendant. The
Dred Scott decision of 1857, which held that Congress had
no power to exclude slavery from individual states and
territories, gave the Confederate States the encouragement
to repeal their grant of powers to the national government
and to secede from the Union.

Since the Civil War, the prevailing sentiment of the American people, as reflected in the Supreme Court's constitutional interpretations, has been to assert national policy over the divergent desires of the states. Most Americans would agree that the special interests of the states should be subordinated to the greater interest of the nation as a whole in the give and take of the political process.

I don't think that the old arguments for "states' rights" are relevant any longer, nor is the end of narrow interpretations of states' rights in any way a limitation of legitimate state power. As much as I believe in the decentralization of authority and even the "reprivatization" of government function wherever possible (a term Peter Drucker has made popular), I think that constitutional provisions dealing with the basic rights of citizenship are not subject to local interpretation. If a state feels strongly enough about certain issues, it has both legislative and judicial recourse at the national level. If these fail, it must bow to the will of the national majority. This is the essential meaning of democracy.

The process of history has shifted the emphasis of our federal system from time to time as the economic, social, and even psychological needs for central authority have risen and ebbed like a tide. But throughout our history, there has never been a clear-cut series of layers of authority as exists, for example, in Canada. Within the limits of their means and inclinations, local communities, the states and the national government have had the capacity to perform most of the same functions at the same time. Author Morton Grodzins has pointed out that the American federal system has never been a system of separated governmental activities, that there has never been a time when it was possible to put neat labels on discrete "federal," "state," and "local" systems. In his descriptive image, our system is a "marble cake" instead of a "layer cake," with powers and responsibilities intermingled.[3]

What made possible the adoption of the Constitution was not semantic trickery that deceived the states into believing they were getting true Federalism as contemplated in the Articles of Confederation. It was an intuitive awareness that in large measure, a centralized authority was necessary to preserve the Union and thereby guarantee the survival of its parts. What is unique about the American experience is its pragmatic approach to all situations and even to constitutions. Even today, what works is far more important to most Americans than how it works, or how it has always worked before.

The challenge to the states now is to use the redundancies of the federal system to their advantage; to accept responsibility, rather than shrugging it off, either to the cities, which are unable to assume it, or the federal government, which is overwhelmed by responsibility already, remote, and unable to respond to it.

I read the history of our federal system, not as a lawyer or a political scientist might, but as an ordinary citizen. From the Articles of Confederation to the most recent decisions of the Supreme Court, I find a continuing struggle to mold and modify the various levels of government so that all the people of America can be dealt with accurately and fairly.

For a variety of reasons, unfortunately, the states have handicapped themselves in asserting a position of parity with the federal government. In many instances, they have weakened their own capacity to act by failing to amend the wording of anachronistic state constitutions, by dodging their responsibilities for their suffering cities, and by failing to adopt realistic taxing policies. Too often, they have limited the attractiveness of state service through unrealistic salary schedules and a bureaucratic superstructure offering little scope for individual creativity and less reward for excellence.

Even in the 1970s, many states still bar their governor from succeeding himself. Many center authority in boards and commissions beyond his control and give him a legislature that meets only once in two years and then for a short time.

As Governor Sanford says, "The state constitutions fairly adequately prevent the governor from committing evil. That was perhaps the intent. They also hinder his attempts to pursue excellence." [4]

With all the roadblocks placed in the way of the states, it is remarkable that they have been as resilient and resourceful as they have. Gradually, the worst vices inherent in state constitutions have been amended. The need for a strong executive has been recognized. Legislative and civil service salaries have been raised, and the biennial orgy of logrolling and bill-passing has been disciplined.

After World War I, the states had their greatest opportunity to develop the kind of concurrent leadership inherent in a "marble cake" definition of American Federalism. "It is one of the happy incidents of the federal system," wrote Supreme Court Justice Louis D. Brandeis, "that a single courageous state may, if its citizens choose, serve as a laboratory and try novel social and economic experiments without risk to the rest of the country." [5] Unfortunately, not enough did.

Under the administrations of Taft, Harding, Coolidge and Hoover, the attitude of Washington was one of "benign neglect." The system appeared to be working well enough without constant interference at the national level. This challenged the states either to take the initiative in social reform or to let nature, which seemed to be smiling on the Republic, take its course. Individual states took the lead in developing new forms of taxation, new ways to

limit corporate power, the first workmen's compensation
laws, wage and hour statutes, industrial and public safety
requirements, pure food and drug laws, and civil rights
legislation. In the years between the end of World War I
and the collapse of the economy in 1929, more than
one-third of the states enacted administrative reorganization plans to make state government more effective by
enlarging its responsibilities and improving its capacity to
act.

As an indication of their assumption of a greater role in
providing for their citizens, the states increased their total
expenditures 500 percent from 1913 to 1929.[6] State debt
also doubled during this time, showing a willingness not
only to spend but, long before its was considered wholly
proper, to go into debt to meet their obligations.

Most of the increased burden of expense went to pay
the burgeoning costs of public education and highway
construction. These were the years when automobile
ownership was going public in a big way and universal
education was rapidly being accepted as a right by all
segments of American society.

As James T. Patterson points out, however, "The most
serious failure of the states was their reluctance to adopt
adequately financed social legislation." [7] Accepting the
prevailing sentiment that "the business of America is
business," the states sank into a numbing lassitude. Even
those like Massachusetts, Wisconsin, and California,
which had served, in Justice Brandeis's terms, as "labora-
tories for novel social and economic experiments," slept
the dreamless sleep. Part-time amateur legislators shuttled
in and out of office averaging no more than two terms. The
great majority of these were not beaten at the polls, but
retired to greener pastures and more lucrative occupations
once they had proved their allegiance either to party or to
the status quo by voting the "right way." Even if they
remained in office, they were part-timers compounded.

Almost half of the state legislatures during this period convened for no more than sixty days in a two-year period, while only five states had annual sessions.

With no pressure to govern in any but the most rudimentary sense, state capitals remained political protectorates of the establishment, and state governments served primarily to preserve and protect the privileges and powers of the dominant economic interests within the state borders.

Although America was shifting rapidly from a rural to an urban society during this period, the states were ill-prepared to cope with the growing problems of the cities. In Washington, the federal government was providing little moral or political leadership in establishing programs designed to meet social change.

Whenever the states seemed to be usurping too much power, the United States Supreme Court could be counted on to overrule state initiatives in areas like wage and hour statutes, price and rate regulations, progressive taxes, and even public expenditures—all areas the court felt beyond the states' power to regulate. To guarantee that state legislatures would be relatively powerless to meet the critical problems of post-war America, state political districting policies greatly favored the rural counties, packing the statehouses with representatives basically disinterested in, and even hostile to, the peculiar needs of swelling urban centers.

Today, impelled by recent Supreme Court decisions and national legislative policy, many of the states have shaken off the do-nothing, know-nothing image of that period. But a pervasive cynicism about the reliability and integrity of state governments still exists. As recently as the late 1950s and 1960s, Governors Faubus of Arkansas and Wallace of Alabama attempted to revive the spirit of nullification by refusing to honor the intent of *Brown v. The Board of Education* when it came to equal opportunity in education. In Montana, school children learn quite young to describe their state as the place where "the mountains are high and the politics are low." In the early 1960s, a researcher for a national organization whose assignment was to analyze progressive social legislation in Missouri returned with the one-sentence comment, "I cannot discover anything that the State of Missouri has done in this field."

Part of the American condescension toward the states is a current national tendency toward self-deprecation. Part is an inability to shake off the stereotypes of the past. In 1949, the reporter Robert S. Allen wrote a muckraking book called *Our Sovereign States*, which began with the often-quoted invective: "State government is the tawdriest, most incompetent, and most stultifying unit of the nation's political structure.[8]

"The whole system," he went on, "is moribund, corrosive, and deadening. It is riddled with senescence, incompetence, mediocrity, ineffectiveness, corruption, and tawdriness. It pollutes instead of purifying, destroys and obstructs instead of building and improving." [9]

When my industrialist friend called state government a graveyard, these were some of the epitaphs he was reading. But he misjudged two important phenomena which have produced, if not a full-fledged resurrection of state government, at least a stirring among the tombstones today and the promise of more sensitive public service tomorrow.

The first is the dawning truth that beyond making broad policy determinations, the federal government cannot design and operate programs which will be applicable and workable at the local level in the increasingly complex society of the 1970s. The second is that over the last decade, there has been a gradual lifting of the pall of mediocrity and impotency which, for too long, veiled the true potential of the states.

State legislatures, as author John Burns points out, have

begun to show new signs of life. "Innovative policies and programs in such fields as education, air and water pollution, mental health, and transportation have begun to emerge. Legislatures have begun to gear themselves to cast off crippling constitutional restrictions, to overhaul their structure and procedures, to have more and better staffs, to meet more often and stay on the job longer, to pay their members better so that they can, in fact, function as one of our more important institutions of government." [10] From my experience in Connecticut, I can verify his conclusions 100 percent.

The shell shock which began with the Depression and continued through World War II, the Fair Deal, the Eisenhower years, the New Frontier, and the Great Society is being shaken off at every level of state government. With 15 million people unemployed by 1933, and major industry closing its doors, thus shutting down the faucet of its tax and purchasing dollars, the states were almost totally paralyzed and looked to Washington not only for reassurance but for action—any action. In Connecticut, crusty old Governor Wilbur Cross struck the colors of Yankee self-reliance when he said: "In the emergency, I am ready to lay aside the unsubstantial ghost of state sovereignty. I am ready to accept funds for the aged, the crippled, for humane and educational institutions, for the extension of highways, and even for the extermination of mosquitoes along the shore." [11]

Today, while still looking to the national government for policies, guidelines, and program dollars, we are not at all sure that the federal agencies can do an adequate job of exterminating the mosquitoes along the Connecticut shore or handling their contemporary equivalents, the gypsy moth and the elm spanworm, or, in fact, that they even care. These functions and most others that deal with purely local issues can best be handled by the people who live in closest intimacy with them. Specific categorical grants-in-aid may be useful in dealing with certain commonly shared problems. But *general revenue sharing*, in my opinion, offers the greatest opportunity for the states to do what they should be able to do best—handle within their own borders the troubles that peculiarly beset their own people. And, to my way of thinking, this includes most of today's problems.

Regardless of the arbitrariness of these state borders or the transiency of our people, the fifty states are a unique combination of human, economic, and environmental assets and liabilities. Although a portion of these assets is held in trust by, and is under the contol of, the national government, the primary role of "asset management" (a term borrowed from my Wall Street days) clearly resides in the individual states themselves. On the human level, these assets consist of the basic rights of every citizen not only to enjoy the Constitutional privileges of life, liberty, and the pursuit of happiness but to have access to equal opportunity in education, health, housing, employment and the use of all the resources of his state to which, as a citizen, he has clear title.

This is why any definition of states' rights which limits the use or enjoyment of states' assets or in any way discriminates against equal opportunities of individuals or groups is just dead wrong. Wherever this occurs, those representatives of state government who tolerate discrimination or who convert state assets to their own use and enjoyment should clearly be put out of business just as if they were "asset managers" found guilty of misappropriating private funds and diverting them to their own purposes.

On the economic level, competition between the states for business, for federal grants, or for any other source of revenue is healthy and worthwhile until it begins to infringe on the efficient management of other types of assets such as air, water, open land, and that intangible but most precious asset called "quality of life." Here, for example, is where environmentalists clash with state development commissions. State government must arbitrate these disputes by establishing a workable system of trade-offs and acceptable norms, which has as its basic blueprint a state land use plan. The federal government, to keep this competition from becoming harmful to overall environmental assets, must establish programs that will help allow the states to be able to sacrifice individual growth and development, when their benefits are outweighed by their damage to the environment.

If there is a New Federalism, it is new only in its emphasis on shared rather than layered responsibility. As the National Commission on Urban Problems reported, "By using the powers they already possess, by assuming new authority where necessary and in providing funds, [the states] occupy a unique position . . . state governments are close to the people and the problems but bring enough perspective to bear to help release urban areas from the excess of localism." [12]

As we begin preparation for our country's two-hundredth anniversary celebration, the states need not be harassed by their somewhat tawdry reputation nor humbled by their lack of power in relation to the federal government. The states and the national government walk together into the second biennium as strong partners.

John Gardner has said that "state government is reputedly a dull subject." This may once have been true. It is true no longer. We have in recent years focused our attention on our nation's tragic war, its moral and economic position in the world, the staggering policy shifts that have occurred, shattering old hostilities and forging new friendships. Now we must begin to turn more of our attention inward to see how well we can sustain our policies abroad by recreating vitality at home.

This struggle will be anything but dull. With national

CHAPTER 3

Making It Work

★

Executives are people who make things work. One way the successful executive functions is to take a complex problem, divide it into manageable segments, think through each segment, and organize to unsnarl these smaller components. Then he is ready to put them all together into a balanced solution. Ideally, this is the way our federal system should function. Viewed from the White House or a Cabinet department, the problems of the United States as a whole often look utterly hopeless. But broken down into a minimum of fifty parts, they seem more amenable to human effort and ultimate resolution.

On the Mississippi River, there are eleven thousand separate sand and gravel pits causing erosion and sedimentation problems along the river. There is no way that the federal bureaucracy can muster enough lawyers, clerks, inspectors, and hearing officers to stop the pollution from each of these sources. But, divided among the states along the river, the problems become relatively manageable. What's more, the interest of each state in the Mississippi's clean water is direct and immediate, while that of the federal government is remote.

The states should be the national government's most important resource for problem solving. That they are not is, in part, due to limitations they have placed upon themselves—a tendency to think small, to settle for mediocrity instead of reaching for outer limits of their powers and resources. It is also due in part to the failure of the federal government to acknowledge states as full-fledged partners.

In exposing the weaknesses of state governments, critics have found no shortage of fat targets. Constitutions are wordy and archaic. Governors are either too weak or too strong. The legislatures, as the Citizens' Conference on State Legislation has pointed out, stand high on the list of institutions that need reform. Or as John McGlennon, the very effective EPA Regional Director in Boston, jokingly —I think—has said, "The only time the citizen is safe is when the legislatures are out of session." State officials and civil servants are grossly underpaid, unappreciated, and, in too many instances, scraped from the bottom of the patronage barrel. State tax systems are often inadequate. The objectives of state government are often petty and selfish, geared to enhancing private interests rather than furthering the public good.

Yet, all these criticisms can be made to apply to any human institution. Churches are often venal. Universities can be intellectually dishonest. Schools are frequently hostile to the needs of their students. Businessmen often put corporate profit ahead of the public good. And on and on.

The states are no better or worse than any other human establishment. One difference, however, is that while we have traditionally placed much faith in churches, schools, and even business, we have tended to depreciate the value of the state and state government. From my own experience, I believe the states can be made to work and work well. Very often the obstacles to effectiveness are not major. Just a little tinkering will sometimes get a stalled engine moving again.

One example among many comes to mind. In the spring of 1971, shortly before the Department of Environmental Protection Act was passed, Connecticut was mandated by the Federal Air Quality Act to develop a comprehensive statewide plan to meet rigorous federal air emission standards. Target date was January 1972, a mere three months after the department was officially in business. In ninety days, we had to develop a plan that would dictate the quality of Connecticut's air for decades to come. I could only echo the sentiments of some of my young colleagues, "Oh, wow."

The resources we inherited from the Department of Health's Air Program were exceedingly slim. Only a small working group had any expertise on the subject and that was tradition-bound. Most of us in the new department, what there were of us, were innocent of the inner workings of the "system," and totally ignorant of the specifics required under the Act.

But state government gave us the authority and flexibility to get the job done. In 1970, I had worked with two very bright young environmentalists in the National Earth Day movement. One was a medical student, Andy Garling, the other a law student, Steve Cotton, both at Harvard. I brought them to Connecticut as "consultants" (in spite of their beards and the skepticism this evoked in the old guard), called together the members of various citizens' committees, alerted every professional group I could think of, assembled the thin human resources of the department, and soon had an effective task force organized to draft and redraft Connecticut's Clean Air Plan and, what's more, to get it out on schedule.

Nothing in the state constitution or the legislation either encouraged us in this approach or barred us from using it. We simply did what needed doing. It was government at its best, I felt, close to the people, calling on the people, and the people responded.

Operating under an austere budget, we had very little in the way of funds. But the citizen groups under the leadership of the Connecticut TB and Respiratory Disease

Association, the professional groups, spearheaded by lawyer Peter Cooper, and the environmental section of the Connecticut Business and Industry Association combined their own resources and were ingenious at helping us get money from the federal government and foundations to conduct needed research, hold regional workshops, public hearings, and group indoctrination sessions on the processes and implementation of the plan.

Within a few weeks, we had a core citizens' committee, composed of scientists, ecologists, physicists, chemists, businessmen, lawyers, and ordinary citizens who gave their services to the state for nothing. In addition, we had an ad hoc committee composed of the air health officials from our ten largest cities, led by Chris Beck, who later joined the department as head of our Air Compliance Section.

When the deadline arrived, we had our plan. It was a good one. It was submitted to the people through public hearings, refined, revised, approved by the governor, and eventually was one of a handful accepted by the Federal Environmental Protection Agency without reservation.

The creaking, unwieldy machinery of the old state bureaucracy was never called into play. We simply bypassed it. Any other state, any other community, could have done the same. The federal government had set a policy and mandated a task. The people of the state gave their consent and the governor lent his authority. The rest was easy—to use the powers which were there waiting to be used and to enlist effectively the capable volunteers so desirous of serving their fellow citizens.

As a postscript, all the ironies of state government descended upon us after completion. As vast a plan as this was, as complex as its provisions were, as difficult as its preparation had been, somehow our first "draft" was being held up in the bureaucracy. Unless it was sent out, we could not get timely federal approval. When it was not out, I could not be sure just what the delay was and sent an emissary to the Environmental Health Office to find out.

When our scout returned, I couldn't believe the answer he gave me. In fact, I can scarcely believe it even today, but it drove home to me the reason why bureaucracies so often come under attack, and rightly so.

Our first draft was stuck in the bureaucracy because we had no rubber stamp for a return address. As we were a brand new agency, we had not received that vital piece of equipment which imprinted, "Department of Environmental Protection." Because it was not a budgeted item, no one could figure out how to solve the problem of obtaining one.

I issued a directive: "Either write out the return address by hand or get a rubber stamp from Public Works within twelve hours." In some buried office, no doubt, a dim, devoted civil servant shook his head sadly, looked around carefully to see that he wasn't being watched, wrote "Department of Environmental Protection" on the envelope, and dropped it into the mailbox.

All foul-ups on the state level are not that simple to repair. But the states have a very adequate tool kit of powers. It's a matter of wanting to get the breakdown fixed as much as having the proper equipment with which to fix it. A good starting place is with the state constitution itself, for it is here that the fears and follies of the past often place the tightest shackles on the willing hands of the present.

The relationships between the states and their local political subdivisions are defined, sometimes clearly, sometimes obscurely by a complex network of statutes, traditions, codes, and constitutional provisions. What makes it so difficult for the states to manage their assets wisely and to minimize their liabilities is not, generally, that they are limited or thwarted by the federal Constitution. As Professor Frank P. Grad points out, "The federal Constitution is a document of grant and delegation, for, in spite of its enormous power, the federal government must trace all its powers to one of several constitutional grants made to it by the original states." [13]

On the other hand, "State constitutions are instruments of limitation." [14] Over the years, state constitutions have become encrusted with the barnacles of old suspicions, fears, and outmoded traditions. Dominant forces in state legislatures have viewed with alarm the economic, cultural, and social changes sweeping over them with increasing force and velocity. Consequently, they have attempted to use the state constitution as a dike to hold back the inevitable ocean of change.

Constitutional authors and succeeding generations of constitutional amenders have seen to it that most state constitutions are relatively rigid, inflexible, and difficult to alter. While the perceptive statesmen who wrote the United States Constitution understood that their document was a frame within which succeeding generations of Americans could depict changing landscapes, most state constitutions are as detailed and finicky as a paint-by-number picture.

Commentators on state government have underscored the wordiness and rigidity of state constitutions. Governor Sanford points out that the Louisiana Constitution is 236,000 words, "at least half as long as *Gone with the Wind*." [15] Like an old inner tube, it has been patched at least three hundred times. In contrast, the federal Constitution, not including the Bill of Rights, has been amended only sixteen times in 185 years, with two of these amendments canceling each other out. Texas recently brought in a 14,000-word revision eliminating most of the legislative detail that has hampered this state's government since a group of Democrats wrote the constitution in 1875, putting every restriction they could think of on the government that had just been wrested from a powerful Republican governor, Edmund J. Davis. Such constitutions were common in the South after Reconstruction and we live with the results today. Charles Ravenal, the exciting Democratic nominee for governor of South Carolina, was challenged twice in two jurisdictions during the campaign of 1974 on an archaic five-year residence requirement for any gubernatorial aspirant—a holdover from law of the Reconstruction era. And South Carolina came out the poorer for his thwarted candidacy.

A model state constitution, prepared by the National Municipal League, contains only 12,500 words, which is still almost three times what it took the laconic Vermonters to say their constitutional piece. But the problem with state constitutions is less their length than the inhibiting spirit in which they were written. Even though the original states had ratified a national Constitution creating a strong central government, post-Revolutionary state politicians still reflected the same fear of strong executive power that had shaped the Articles of Confederation. And we live with that today, too.

In addition, as growth of American business and industry sorely tempted state politicians to feather their own nests by selling, exploiting, or giving away state lands and resources, state constitutions began to be amended to reflect a distrust of legislative power. As Professor Grad says, "The early twentieth century brought a fear of representative democracy generally and increased reliance on direct democracy, initiative, referendum, and recall. The fear of the immigrant city population brought with it greater restriction on voting rights reflected in longer residency requirements. The majority of state constitutions reflect these successive layers of fear, severely limiting the state governments' freedom of action." [16]

Because state constitutions have traditionally reflected the biases of rural, "down-state" interests, their lack of flexibility has been most severely felt in dealing with urban problems. In many cases, state constitutions fiddle while the cities burn. Constitutional restrictions on state and local taxing and borrowing power, as well as specific limitations on the structures and power of local government, have left the states unable to handle the rising costs of meeting the problems of the cities.

Another of the states' difficulties in carrying out sensible asset management is the proliferation of local government with the accompanying diffusion of power, prerogatives, and responsibilities. Each of the 268 so-called SMSAs (Standard Metropolitan Statistical Areas) in the United States is divided into an average of ninety-one local governments. Each of these manages and controls (or mismanages and loses control of) a portion of the resources within these areas. Although the number of subdivisions varies sharply, the confusion of proliferating local government may be judged by the fact that at least one SMSA is divided into more than 1,100 local units, and many others are not far behind.

In Connecticut, the five thousand square miles of state assets are distributed among 169 villages, towns, and cities. Most of these are rural in character. Only a few can be called cities in the accepted sense and the largest of these cities has roughly 150,000 residents. Connecticut's traditional county structure was eliminated through constitutional reform in 1959. Not that the counties ever did any real political managing. County commissioners whom no one could name were appointed by a malapportioned legislature and given municipal responsibilities. With the movement of population, traditional county seats lost whatever significance they had possessed.

Yet today, despite the official termination of county government, the people of Connecticut still think, in part, in county terms and resort to artificial synonyms like "region" or "planning district" to express what the old county idea embodied. And throughout the United States county government is undergoing a rejuvenation with highly professional county executives and county managers providing a significant layer of government between the community and the state. In some areas, Indianapolis, Indiana, and Nashville, Tennessee, for example, county and city governments have merged. This, in effect, removes that added layer of government while, at the same time, strengthens the governmental entity that remains.

These natural groupings of community interest should be given very careful consideration by the states. For, as the states themselves are to the federal government, so these resource clusters are to the states. Good asset management involves distribution of executive responsibility and control to the most natural groupings of common interest which are small enough to be responsive to the people and large enough to bring sufficient resources to bear on local problems.

Just as the national government is too big and remote to control the discharge of every sand and gravel pit on the Mississippi, so the states, especially the larger states, do not have the capacity to fill every pothole in a local thoroughfare or review the curriculum of every junior high school. As a general rule, problems should be solved and services delivered at the level of the "lowest common denominator."

During the late 1960s, when the states were beginning to recognize their inability to cope with the massive problems of poverty, urbanization, transportation, education, and the rest, there was a renaissance of constitutional reform in the states. Between 1966 and 1972, two-thirds of all the states were involved in some constitutional reform. Ten more had already held constitutional conventions or had organized constitutional commissions between 1950 and 1966.

One of the sharpest stimuli to constitutional reform was

the mandate for reapportionment which the states were forced to meet through the Supreme Court's reinterpretation of the federal Constitution. Even beyond this though, the states began to recognize, poignantly throughout the reform years of the 1960s, that the federal government was not going to be able to perform as advertised in Great Society press releases.

Federal attempts to bypass the statehouse and to pinpoint funds in cities or even neighborhoods under federal control created the appearance of change. But most often, the ultimate reality was fiscal and substantive "bankruptcy" and programmatic chaos. Local political units are too small to generate the critical mass necessary to keep programs going *unless* the resource generators of the state are also wired in and understand.

In a handful of cities, like New York, Chicago, or Los Angeles, political subdivisions are as large as some states. These I believe, must be treated as special cases and handled by a different kind of resource management—a joint venture of national, state, city, and community interests. The spectacle of internecine warfare, as practiced by the Governor of New York and the Mayor of New York City in times past, while understandable, has done nothing to add luster either to their careers or to the science of government. And it certainly hasn't served the citizens of New York, either the city or the state.

In the case of New York City, it alone has a critical mass which makes it incapable of control by the state, whose total resources are not as great and whose needs are far less concentrated. While, to some extent, the 1969 mayoralty campaign of Norman Mailer and Jimmy Breslin may have been a journalistic lark, these creative candidates did pose one highly charged question which never received a satisfactory answer.

Should New York City be permitted to secede and to constitute itself as a separate state? I am not certain how the question should be answered. But I do know that perhaps short of statehood, there must be a better response to that city's problems than the game of manipulation, one-upmanship, and mutual insensitivity that has been played for decades between the chief executives of city and state. In the larger metropolitan areas, this question is crucial—and delay in answering it could well be fatal.

Beyond the few largest cities, however, America's urban and suburban areas can be incorporated conveniently into statewide policies and programs of asset management. State constitutions, though, must be made flexible enough to permit the modernization of state policy in respect to urbanization, population growth, mobility, technological development, land use, borrowing and taxing, the pressures for equal treatment of minority groups, and other significant issues that must be resolved in the last quarter of the twentieth century.

Constitutional reform, as hammered out in conventions, is not the end of the process of change, but just the beginning. *The Book of The States* points to an alarming drop in adoptions of constitutional changes proposed during the 1970–71 biennium. Unless the legislative and executive leadership is able to communicate effectively the need for such change, the voters may be wary of adopting reform which they feel may place heavier economic or social responsibilities upon them, and which they may not fully understand.

In Louisiana, for example, recent balloting for fifty-three constitutional amendments drew only 23 percent of the registered voters to the polls and resulted in the defeat of all fifty-three amendments. From 1966 to 1972, voters in eight states cast ballots on new constitutions; only two were passed. Throughout all the states, constitutional reform by legislative proposal has become the most popular and successful method of change. This places an added burden of responsibility on the state legislatures to be responsive and responsible, two virtues with which they have not generally been credited in the past. But, let's look at the legislatures of today.

Robert S. Allen is no more sparing of the state legislative bodies than he is of state government itself. "The legislatures are the bawdy houses of state government," he says. "Without exception, legislatures, as a whole, are a shambles of mediocrity, incompetence, hooliganism, and venality. They are the most sordid, destructive, and antidemocratic law-making agencies in the country." [17] Quite a charge!

Written in 1949, this harsh invective, which echoes generations of reformist scorn, is far less applicable today than it might have been then. State legislatures may not be populated by selfless paragons, but increasingly they are attracting men and women of probity and concern, who take quite literally their title of "representative of the people." True, at times we may accomplish more when they aren't in session, but the people of the states are certainly well-served, both individually and collectively, when they are. I know, from my own dealings with Connecticut's representatives, they are serving their constituents every day and serving them well.

Before the pressure for reapportionment, culminating in the crucial decision of *Baker v. Carr,* the legislatures of most states were created largely by obsolete districting, designed to serve powerful special interests. Even today, we hear of the oil and gas interests of Louisiana, the insurance interests of Connecticut, the mining and power interests of Montana, and the concentration of corporate influence which, it is argued, has made Delaware little more than a branch office of the Du Pont Corporation.

David Broder, in his pungent book *The Party's Over,* recalls "standing in the back of the Texas House of Representatives while the speaker of the body, who had been named as a key figure in a stock fraud scheme, gaveled through two dozen bills in ten minutes while the 'Dirty Thirty,' as the few maverick legislators were called, frantically flashed their voting board lights red to protest this travesty on the legislative process." [18]

I believe it would be as mistaken to permit these stereotypes of corrupt state government to represent the current reality as to permit Smokey the Bear to stand as a symbol of America's environmental awareness today. There's much more to it than that.

Just as in each of us there are baser elements, so there are vestiges of sloppiness, corruption, venality, and reaction in every state legislature. But from my own experience with the legislature of Connecticut, I can only sound a note of encouragement and optimism.

It's not that humanity is becoming more perfect or more amenable to rule by law. Reapportionment according to the theory of "one man, one vote" has been influential in producing structural change and breaking up old, entrenched power blocks no longer representative of the numbers and types of people actually living within the state. Other factors are even more responsible for bringing about a heightened quality of leadership within the halls of state government. One of these is increased salaries, which have made it possible for a broader cross section of the states' citizens to run for political office. Another is the growing participation of youth, women, minority groups, and others who have been grossly underrepresented in the past. Another is the heightened level of awareness and concern of most citizens with the problems of the day and their sincere desire to contribute their share to solving them.

A combination of increased salaries, greater mobility, and heightened participation has permitted more people in the helping professions, such as social workers, doctors, nurses, and educators, to decide to make either a second or even a primary career of politics. As one Connecticut legislator told me, "These women who are becoming full-time legislators are among the best we have. They take their job seriously. They're not easily influenced by narrow lobbyists. They really believe government should help the people."

Frances (Sissy) Farenthold, although defeated for the Texas governorship, is an excellent example of an effective state legislator. Her leadership of the "Dirty Thirty" within the Texas House of Representatives, and her campaign for governor in 1972, stimulated a surge of reform which radically changed the personnel and leadership of that state legislature; it also pressed Texas toward a badly needed new constitution. Connecticut has numerous examples of distaff legislative leadership in such women as Mary Griswold, wife of the late president of Yale, Florence Finney, Senate President Pro Tem with twenty-five years in the Connecticut legislature, and, of course, a former member of the legislature, Governor Ella Grasso, the first woman to be elected governor of an American state in her own right.

Another cause for legislative improvement, and to me a most significant one, is the growing sense of public responsibility among business organizations. In greater numbers each year, corporations are encouraging employees to become involved in public service, including government, and giving them time off the job to run for office or participate otherwise in the political process. In the Department of Environmental Protection, we were given the loan of a full-time employee by IBM, Bob Timbers by name. He was an excellent man, extremely effective and not someone IBM could easily spare. We almost recruited a vice-president from Xerox as well, but lost out to the Pueblo Indians. Some of the state's best legislators, like Senator Sam Hilliard from General Dynamics, are on leaves of absence from state-based businesses.

Beyond these internal reasons for better legislatures, I

believe the average citizen is fed up with bumbling, dishonest government. He will no longer stand by passively, while both the human and physical resources of his state are cynically ripped off by personal prejudice and private greed. Also, the newspapers, radio, and TV of the states have been an important factor in educating the citizens to the facts of life in state government. Although coverage of the Statehouse is not as comprehensive or in-depth as it might be, and some coverage is downright prejudiced and distorted, a new generation of reporters is elbowing aside the jaded old Statehouse hacks who once willingly performed public relations favors for a bottle or a buck. Connecticut has some of the most outstanding representatives of this new breed, I discovered.

In at least two states, newspaper and broadcast coverage of the legislature has been supplemented by magazine coverage that is aggressive and generally honest. The *Texas Observer* is both a goad and an irritant to state legislators of the old school, while *New York* Magazine has provided some of the most pungent coverage of that state's legislative sessions. In my own state, a new publication, *Connecticut Magazine*, has begun to zero in on state politics with some excellent investigative reporting— which, at the very least, is calculated to keep the politicians awake.

As an aside, however, this new style is not always on the plus side of the ledger. Practitioners of advocacy reporting often make life miserable for members of the governmental establishment who have been accustomed to operating in the shadows. Yet, in their anxiety to make a headline or their zeal to expose malfeasance, these highly charged journalists too often rely on leaks, rumors, and "inside sources" which, in their own way, can be as dishonest and misleading as press handouts, exclusives, and paid puffs.

In addition, there is a muckraking establishment which has become as bureaucratized in its own way as the governmental establishment. Well-meaning and highly motivated, these private organizations and individuals depend for their survival on high visibility and the capacity to create continuous shock waves. Very often this results in overreaching and a sense of self-righteousness that makes everything they do not agree with seem somehow tainted and suspect in their eyes. Typical of this arrogance and disdain for individual rights is the playing of a subpoenaed tape by a Nader lawyer at a Georgetown cocktail party.

In Connecticut, a prime example of this type of effort is the Connecticut Citizens Action Group, another Nader affiliate, which combines public service and self-service in equal quantities. Its former head, Toby Moffett, used the "consumer advocate" platform to run for Congress in Connecticut's Sixth District. After blasting every ap- pointed official he could think of (including me) for using the position as a stepping-stone to elective office, he blithely did precisely that. I only wish the dedicated men and women of these groups could be more balanced and mature in evaluation and response. Then they would truly serve the citizen.

Impatience with evil may be a shining virtue. But in government, one rarely deals in issues that are clear-cut, black or white. Often we must take the time to sort through various shades of gray. The new activist organiza- tions and their associates in the media are keenly aware that it's the black versus the white which attracts attention, makes headlines, and sells. This, then, is the way they often interpret every action and decision of government. Perhaps there's no alternative. Maybe change can only come about under the prodding of absolutists. But it would be comforting to know that the good, gray center is also capable of producing change in a climate of civility.

I remember vividly the day that one of the most ardent

environmentalists in Connecticut came into my office to enlist my support for her very visible and audible fight against highways, specifically the proposed I-291 circumferential route around Hartford. I spent a half hour telling her why we were initiating a pioneering land-use/transportation study for the Capitol region. Why couldn't we say flat out that we were against all projected highways? "It will take time," I said, "but we'll get the answers. And they will guide us in helping to set transportation policies which are most protective of the environment, in harmony with past and proposed land use, yet meet legitimate citizen transportation needs now. And these, in turn, can serve as a benchmark for the state."

Her expression never changed. "So you're *not* against the highway," she said flatly.

"I didn't say that," I replied, somewhat irritated. And I went through it all again. I might as well have been talking to a highway. "So you're *for* the road," she said when I had finished.

"I don't know where I am. I'm trying to answer the question of what's best for the citizens." I told her again that we were investing a million dollars in a first-in-the-nation land-use/transportation study.

When I got all finished she just looked at me and said, "You're not *against* the road; therefore you're *for* the road." And that's the way she reported it to her contacts in the media. Perhaps there's no other way.

Environmental, population, consumer, and racial activists have been indispensable to the improvement of state government. Their energetic refusal to compromise has done much to push the bureaucracy off dead center. But too much pressure to act without thought, according to some prearranged scenario, can lead to paralysis of leadership just as surely as lack of pressure and inertia can lead to drift in leadership. On balance, though, I welcome the activists. Even when they have clamored for my head, I have been convinced that their motives were reasonably pure even if their zeal was unreasonably excessive.

Although man for man and woman for woman the quality of state legislators is getting better rapidly, it is extremely difficult for them to function effectively under the conditions prevailing in most states. Salaries are only part of the problem. Lack of adequate staffs, research facilities, and legislative program development personnel cripple even the best intentioned legislators. Beyond these impediments, even when they want to get things done, legislators often find it impossible to concentrate on effective law-making amidst the mishmash of hearings, committee meetings, lobbying pressures, and eleventh-hour voting sessions, which dispose of literally hundreds of bills in the ridiculously short time most state constitutions allow for each legislative outing.

Each Connecticut senator, for example, has an average of seven committee assignments. If he took this burden literally and tried to divide himself seven ways, no intelligible business would ever get done at all. As it is, most legislation is written not by the legislators themselves but in the government departments and commissions responsible for the areas of state government covered by the legislation. Fortunately, in Connecticut, a pool of legislative technicians is now available so that the overextended commission staffs as well as the members of the legislature can have professional help in drafting the bills whose passage they are seeking in the current session.

Other states involved in improving their state legislatures include Arkansas, which streamlined its committee structure, consolidating twenty-five standing committees to ten. In 1973, Louisiana held the first of what is expected to be an annual series of presession conferences to acquaint legislators with the issues before the session, and six states and the District of Columbia used federal grants to finance automated information systems for coordinating legislative activities.

Yet without question, the model of excellence in state legislatures is the California legislature where "Big Daddy" Jess Unruh, former speaker of the state assembly, literally reshaped and professionalized the legislative branch of government.

As Neal R. Peirce reports in *The Megastates of America*, "The great strength of California [is] its superbly staffed, full-time, well-paid legislature . . . Unruh gave the assembly the tools it needed to handle research and program development, largely through high-grade professional staffs assigned to the committees—probably the best of any of the states. Individual legislators were also given budgets for staff assignments, administrative assistants, secretaries, and field representatives—reminiscent of the U.S. Congress. And they were accorded a new measure of independence by the highest legislative salaries in the United States, with another several thousand dollars each year in fringe benefits." [19]

With more states moving toward annual legislative sessions, and demands on legislators' time becoming greater, more states are following the lead of California. In 1973, five states raised both legislators' salaries and allowances (Georgia, Illinois, New York, Wisconsin, and Wyoming); Ohio and Washington (in addition to California) increased salaries; and Montana, North Dakota, and Pennsylvania hiked expense accounts. But the range of state legislators' salaries is still rather wide—from $100 a year in New Hampshire to $26,745 in California. The average is $8,442.[20]

Through this dramatic upgrading of the human and material resources of the state legislature, individual lawmakers are given the opportunity to supplement educational efforts of lobbyists and to acquire the basic information needed to understand the legislation in which they are involved as well as the procedures necessary to its passage. In many states, paid lobbyists are the only sources of such information. While this is not all bad, lobbyists usually are not all-encompassing or unbiased, which leads to distortion if not misrepresentation.

Not every state has sufficient resources to upgrade its legislature so drastically. Moreover, the public is not always favorably inclined to support increases in legislative pay and perquisites. But every state can do *something*, and most states are. Not only is legislative modernization being carried out on a large scale, including upgrading of salaries, providing for annual sessions, increasing their length, and authorizing greatly enlarged staffs, but, perhaps even more important, the legislatures are rejecting their old "bawdy house" image. In most states, they are enacting stringent laws pertaining to conflict of interest, financial reporting, legislative ethics, regulation of lobbyists, reporting of contributions, and, in general, tightening the old moral loopholes through which lobbyists, special interests, and politicians wriggled to consort with one another in private.

In the 1969–70 biennium alone, thirty-two out of fifty states had bills before them calling for some kind of rule change dealing with legislative behavior. The toughest of all conflict-of-interest laws is Maryland's, which requires public disclosure of all relevant financial records such as tax returns. In Connecticut, where lawyers have traditionally dominated the legislature, the conflict-of-interest rule is so strict that it is now a violation of the law for even a member of the legislator's law firm to argue before any of five major commissions so long as his associate is in the House or Senate. To date, however, legislators' salaries paid from previous law partnerships are still condoned.

But, to me, the single greatest strength, by a long measure, of the state legislature is its responsiveness to the voters of the state. And that, of course, is the ultimate source of the strength of state government. As a citizen, you can write your Congressman and even the President. It may or may not get to him, much less change his mind or his vote. But on the state level, the voice of the voter is the voice of a neighbor, far more compelling than an unknown signature on a letter or a telegram. It can be a telephone call to a representative's home, or a conversation at the barber shop or a Cub Scout meeting, or an argument at a legislative committee hearing, or a confrontation in force at a legislator's office. It's not some disembodied "Vox Populi," but the angry roar of the people down the street whom the politician can't avoid until just before the next Election Day. Above all else, this "people power" which I've seen working at the state level has strengthened and reinforced my faith in representative government.

In the very first legislative session in which our new department was involved, we were harried, rushed, harassed, and had no formal program put together. But there were a few key areas in which we were vitally interested and reasonably well informed. One of them was protection of the state's inland wetlands. In the previous session, the Connecticut Scenic Rivers Bill, which had some of the same environmental goals, had failed miserably. Since we had been successful in reinforcing and extending excellent tidal wetlands legislation for Connecticut, we decided that our major priority after that was inland wetlands, a rather broad definition of 20–25 percent of the entire state's land mass. Our immediate problem was that no one on the Environmental Committee knew what an inland wetland was. Even when they were informed, there were grave problems in the definition and administration of the bill since the heart of the legislation was the ability of each community to deter landowners from using these defined lands in ways contrary to good environmental sense.

Though I met regularly and often with the Environmental Committee, serious objections remained. We brought together the key leadership of both parties, but they agreed on one thing only—that the bill was in serious trouble. Then, behind and in front of the scenes, the citizens got to work—the Connecticut Conservation Association, The Connecticut Audubon Society, the League of Women Voters, the Junior Leagues, the County Soil Conservation groups, the various sportsman's groups, the town Conservation Commissions, and private individuals and other groups who were convinced that inland wetlands were a basic resource for the state's long-term environmental welfare.

The key legislator was Jack Prete, at that time co-chairman of the Environmental Committee. All the way through the hearings, the meetings, the late evening discussions, he kept telling me he was against the bill. He wouldn't vote for it under any circumstances. Then, in the last week, citizens began calling his home and sending him telegrams. Finally, he said if there was this kind of support from Connecticut citizens, there was no way he could *not* vote for the bill. He did, and it passed. Not the best bill in the world, as it is a most difficult subject indeed for legislation—a law that needed amending in the next session—but a significant step towards protecting a key, but often disregarded, state asset. Why did it pass? In part, because one legislator, responsive to the lobby of the people, gave the bill his support and his vote—despite his opposition to many of its provisions.

In vital issues like health, drugs, or the environment, it is sometimes hard to remember that the legislature is a political institution in which party interest can lead to petty conflicts. Before reapportionment, it was much simpler for one party or one region or class of citizens to dominate the legislature. Reapportionment has given a new voice to groups and individuals who previously were silent. With one man, one vote, the legislator has a better feeling for his constituency. He recognizes that he must depend for reelection on performance, not on gerrymandering, phony districting, or ward politics.

Connecticut is a politically sophisticated state. For more than a quarter of a century, Democratic Party leadership has been in the hands of John Bailey, former Democratic national chairman under John Kennedy, and that's the political big leagues. Republicans, who have been a minority party in one or both houses of the legislature since the Kennedy years, captured both houses in the Nixon sweep of 1972. Yet, in both Democratic and Republican controlled sessions, and with a tough and controversial, but effective, governor, who did not win, or try to win, the approval of his political adversaries, the Environmental Committee was bipartisan and essentially apolitical on the important issues of water, air, solid waste, enforcement, land use, and all the other pressing, but potentially divisive, environmental concerns of the state.

In our first session, the administration was Republican, but the majority in the legislature was Democratic. In the second session, both houses of the legislature became Republican. But it made no difference. I was particularly gratified to hear (although others may not have been) that one of the committee members, in briefing new legislators, emphasized that in issues of the environment, it didn't matter whether you were a Republican or a Democrat. "The Department of Environmental Protection," he said, "treats you the same way and gives you the same information. You can count on it." Both parties recognized the importance of this committee by appointing their brightest people to it. Guided by a nonpartisan intelligence and concern, committee members were dedicated, hardworking, and immensely patient in inching their way through extremely difficult technical matters which didn't lend themselves to easy solutions or to political grandstanding.

One of the most important steps in improving the quality of the legislative process was the reduction in the number of standing committees from twenty-nine to nineteen. Every committee is joint, so that both senators and house members are represented. Senators are given seven committee assignments and house members generally have three or four. With this streamlining of legislative jurisdictions—combined with the beginning of better staffing and a more professional approach—I believe the Connecticut State Legislature, like so many of its counterparts elsewhere, is creating a new respect for state government and a better deal for Connecticut's citizens.

Frank Trippett, in a book critical of the states published in 1967, says that the true constituency of the state legislatures is the business community. Governor Sanford attributes some of the movement of power from states to the federal government to the fact that too many legislatures could not withstand the pressures or blandishments of powerful economic interests within their states. At another point in our history, this may have been true. And in some states where oil, copper, coal, chemicals, or power are king, the vestiges of economic domination may still exist.

But I firmly believe that in the 1970s, one of the reasons for the pressure for return of power from the federal government to the states is the reality that while large multinational conglomerates can perhaps influence the federal establishment, the diffusion of economic power among the states has left them relatively free from excessive business pressure. ITT, the milk marketers, and the energy companies, to name but a few, have sought and found their most significant political constituencies at the federal, and not the state, level.

Most large corporations today have plants, facilities, home and branch offices scattered throughout many states. They can no longer depend on one product or one process for their income or profitability. Paralleling this movement has been the diversification of economic interests within the states. All manner of industries now make their homes in every region. For the most part, there is no single concentration of power large enough to lean on and control an entire legislature or to "own" the Executive or Judicial branch of state government. The "influence" scandals of the 1960s and the 1970s were national in scope reflecting the extent to which federal policy, not state regulation, was crucial to the apparent success of some industries.

At the state level, there are competing and often mutually exclusive interests among the major industries located there. Connecticut's taxing policies may be acceptable to its manufacturing concerns, but not to its insurance companies. Banks and insurance companies are strong advocates of environmental protection, whereas heavy industry sometimes tries to fight clean air and water regulations. Competing lobbyists swarm over the State Capitol; but while there are always rumors of a deal to pass or defeat a certain piece of legislation, these reports are, I am convinced, highly exaggerated. If the citizens take an interest in pending legislation, the special-interest lobbies cannot prevail.

Recently devised regulations concerning campaign financing are contributing to the increasing accountability of state legislators. In Connecticut, for example, campaigns for state office are limited in total expenditures. Individual contributions are, in turn, limited to five thousand dollars, and provision is made for accurate and timely reporting of all receipts and expenditures *before*, not after, election day. Delaware, Maryland, New York, and a host of other states are considering—and passing— similar reforms.

I have been very much impressed with the relative independence of Connecticut's able corps of legislators.

Characteristic of their dedication to the public welfare was their act in a recent session, when Connecticut, with one of the largest and most aggressive groups of negligence lawyers in the nation, became one of a handful of states to pass an effective no-fault insurance law. True, the state's insurance interests favored the bill, but trial lawyers far outnumber insurance men in the ranks of the legislature. Although to most of them no-fault was a significant bread-and-butter issue, they voted overwhelmingly against their bread and butter, in what they were convinced was the public interest.

A dedicated, honest legislature, no less than a modern, flexible constitution, is essential to the modern functioning state. But I believe the absolutely indispensable ingredient of good government at any level is a strong, effective governor. Assuming he's both of the foregoing, how does he work?

In analyzing those factors which contribute to the success of any business organization, management capability comes first. Plant and equipment, patents, marketing organization, research, and financial strength are all items of great importance. But without sound management and inspirational leadership, even the most successful commercial enterprises founder. The chief executive sets the tone of any organization. If he is a strong and active executive, both his substance and his style permeate every level of responsibility and performance. If he is weak, there is a division of authority and an inevitable struggle for domination which fragments and confuses the organization.

This is especially true, I believe, in state government, where the governor is close enough to the people to be observed as an individual, not viewed from a distance as a demigod. One of our problems as a nation is the way we have separated our President from ourselves, endowing him with pomp and panoply more appropriate to royalty than to down-to-earth democracy. With his aides, helicopters, airplanes, homes, military and civilian advisors, secret service men, uniformed guards, ruffles and flourishes, the ever-present and awesome "black box," and the constant prodding of protocol to be something more than ordinary, the President rises above the commonplace. There he is, floating above us, bobbing and swooping gracefully against the sky. Somehow we feel that this huge person should be the embodiment of our strength.

So the President rules—and, as the Watergate case demonstrated, if any hint of a scandal reaches his door, it is not simply a problem of human scale, but a full-fledged Constitutional crisis.

The governor of a state is very much a part of the landscape of the ordinary. Although he may live in a "mansion" in the state capital, his residence is usually far from being the largest or even the most ornate house in town. Some mansions, in fact, are so dilapidated that the governors can't occupy them. In at least seven states, no mansion at all is provided.

In salary, too, the governors of our states are scaled down to human size. The highest gubernatorial salary in the country is New York's $85,000, which is far from the highest salary in that state overall. In fact, some local officials, such as superintendents of schools or top health officers, make almost as much. The lower level gubernatorial salaries range from $10,000 to $25,000—wages which few self-respecting plumbers, if you'll excuse the reference, would settle for today.

Not only do we treat the governor with less than regal emoluments, most states even deny him sufficient powers to be a strong executive. Whereas the President of the United States runs on a short ballot, together with his Vice President, most of our governors are subject to the whims of the electorate, which can saddle him with a lieutenant governor, a secretary of state, a treasurer, or an attorney general of the adversary party.

Our Constitution now limits the President of the United States to two four-year terms. Seventeen states, following the federal model, also limit the governor to two four-year terms. But another nine of our states assure noncontinuity of leadership by insisting that the governor serve only one four-year term, which can lead to such anomalies as Lurleen Wallace succeeding her husband in the statehouse, while he governed from a back room. Four other states weaken the governor by forcing him to run for reelection every two years.

And this caution has its price. In the early spring of 1973, Governor Tom McCall of Oregon made his "grasping wastrels" speech in favor of what was to be Senate Bill 100, Oregon's far-reaching and landmark land-use legislation. But the impact of his extensive environmental experience and his great sense of humanity was weakened by the fact that he was, at the time, a lame-duck governor—Oregon's constitution allows only two four-year terms.

Such limitations reflect the historic distaste of the states for concentrations of executive power. But New York State long ago cast aside any limitation and consequently has been able to establish a record of perhaps the strongest executive management of any of the fifty states. Since 1933, there have been only four elected governors of the state of New York, two Republicans and two Democrats. Each was a man of tremendous individual capability, who also served the national government with distinction. Governor Herbert Lehman served for ten years and went on to become a respected senator. Thomas E. Dewey served twelve years and, during this time, was twice nominated as the Republican candidate for the presidency. Averell Harriman served a four-year term and, both before and after, had a most distinguished career as a public servant. And, of course, Nelson Rockefeller, the senior governor of the nation and one of the most effective, resigned to devote himself to significant national goals prior to his appointment as Vice-President. Going back another decade would bring the total of New York's governors up to only six. Both of these men stopped being governor when they sought the presidency, successfully in the case of Franklin Delano Roosevelt and unsuccessfully in the case of Al Smith.

In a farsighted constitutional change in the 30s, New York called for gubernatorial elections in the off years for four-year terms. Undoubtedly, this has been a major factor in the stability of the statehouse in Albany. New York's governors are elected without reference to national political trends and, further, a governor of New York can run for the presidency without giving up the governor's mansion if he should lose.

In contrast to New York, nearby Pennsylvania has had eleven governors during the years since 1933 (it had four-year terms, but, until 1973, barred reelection), while New Jersey (which now allows a governor a second, but not a third, consecutive term) has had nine governors.

Generally, states are tending to lengthen the terms of the governors and to allow them to run for reelection. Whereas in 1960 there were sixteen states which limited their chief executive to two-year terms, now only four fall into that category: New Hampshire, Rhode Island, Vermont, and Arkansas.

In some states, the governors lack any real power over the budget-making process; in others, the governor's administrative powers are blunted by the coexistence of commissions and boards, often dominated by appointees of a previous governor whose terms run well into the new administration. In still other states, the governor lacks the veto, or has limited appointive powers.

Usually, governors are not the only state official elected statewide. In fact, only in New Jersey does the governor have this distinction. In some states, such as Alaska, both a governor and a lieutenant governor are elected on the same slate. Many states have a pattern like that of New York and Maryland, where the voters elect a governor, a lieutenant governor, a comptroller and an attorney general. Some, like Connecticut, add a secretary of state to this roster. This practice often leads to friction, particularly if the governor belongs to one party, and one or more of the other officials to another. (Both Governor Rockefeller and Governor Meskill faced this problem during their respective tours of duty in the statehouse.)

In Florida, it is even worse; in that state, the voters elect the governor and lieutenant governor (same ticket); the attorney general, comptroller, treasurer, secretary of state, the commissioner of education, commissioner of agriculture, the seven members of the State Supreme Court as well as the three members of the public service commission (a utility regulatory agency). Texas voters still elect a land commissioner and a railroad commissioner (who "regulates" the oil interests), and Louisiana elects a state custodian of voting machines. In days gone by, before New York narrowed its list of statewide elective officials, it used to elect, among others, the surveyor-general. (Even the reform-minded Socialist Party of the 1920s felt honor-bound to go along with this arrangement and dutifully recruited a Socialist surveyor to run for the office.)

Whenever authority is separated from responsibility, inaction and drift result. A chief executive officer in name only is, in some ways, worse for a state than a fool or a charlatan who has the authority, but uses it unwisely. For at least the basic machinery of government can ultimately set to right the mistakes of a governor of broad authority who is a fool. An ambitious, capable executive who finds the reins of government in other hands can be destructive in his frustration.

But this picture is changing. And the change is being brought about largely by a new breed of governor. Far from being party hacks, these men and women are seasoned, capable administrators, many with experience in the private sector, who are aware that the tide of political power is flooding back to the states and are ready and willing to take up this challenge.

Yet it is a reflection of the relatively low estate of the statehouse that the last governor who became President of the United States was elected to his first term over forty years ago. In fact, of the eight Presidents elected in this century before 1940, five—McKinley, Wilson, Coolidge and the two Roosevelts—previously governed their states. Harry Truman, who succeeded Franklin Roosevelt, had been a senator. After him came a military hero who twice defeated a former governor for office. And, after Dwight Eisenhower, three former senators in succession—Kennedy, Johnson, and Nixon—were elected to the White House. Not only that, but all six of the major party nominees since 1960—Kennedy, Johnson, Nixon, Goldwater, Humphrey, and McGovern—came from the Senate and not from the statehouse.

With the apparent resurgence of prestige for state government, some of the ablest contenders for high national office seem to be fighting their preliminaries in the gubernatorial ring. It is difficult to say when one of them will be ready for the main event. Certainly Wallace of Alabama was in the ring slugging away as an active candidate for the presidency in 1972 until his tragic shooting. Reagan of California, Rockefeller of New York, Askew of Florida, Lucey of Wisconsin, and McCall of Oregon have all been mentioned for national office.

More than twenty years ago, the late Senator Richard

Neuberger of Oregon said, "There are few ambitious citizens today who would prefer a governorship to a seat in the U.S. Senate. This is demonstrated by the fact that nearly a third of the present Senate consists of erstwhile governors. . . . What has happened?" he asked. "The governorship was once a political climax." And he answered his own question. "But state government has not been up to the triple challenge of the great Depression, global war, and rocketing inflation. The problems created by these events have been far beyond its scope. Anchored though the federal government may be by tradition and checks and balances, it has the agility of a ballet troupe contrasted with the forty-eight states." [21] In the early 1970s, we are seeing signs of a clear reversal of this trend.

Capable lawmakers like Meskill of Connecticut, Gilligan of Ohio, Moore of West Virginia, and Carey of New York chose to leave the House of Representatives for the statehouse to find a more challenging arena in which to display their executive skills. And in Illinois an effective newcomer to politics, Dan Walker, chose to make his debut as a star in Springfield rather than as a member of the supporting cast in Washington, D.C.

Whatever the reasons, the new emergence of the governors is an encouraging omen for the future of our federal system. Although we are now seeing some signs of change, five years of a President seeking strong central control have proven how little influence senators really have over foreign policy, and how impotent both houses of the national Congress can be in asserting their prerogatives over those of the Executive branch. On the other hand, a strong governor, with his state in a relatively solid financial position, can have the satisfaction of knowing that, for better or for worse, much of what happens within his state happens because of him.

*   *   *

It is not enough, however, to rewrite state constitutions, reform legislatures, or revitalize the authority of the governor. All the working parts of state government can be polished, oiled, and spinning smoothly, but state government will still not function unless it has a direction and a goal; a direction and a goal which benefit the majority of the citizens of the state. If these are absent, then the machinery of government is merely machinery, whizzing efficiently in the corner—all hum and glitter—with no relation at all to the human beings it has been constructed to serve.

Herbert Kramer, a Hartford businessman of great conscience, who was a part of many of the Great Society programs during the 1960s, has told me that he is fearful of revenue sharing for one reason and one reason only: "No one seems to have an adequate understanding of the incentives that motivate a governmental bureaucracy." In dealing with private enterprise, he knows where the pressure points are. He understands that all sorts of diverse motivations are ultimately weighed in the balance of the bottom line.

But, in government, managing to show a surplus is not enough. Neither is getting reelected. For government at any level to work, we need the kind of leadership whose motivation and direction are founded on two basic principles: alleviating the general ills of society and creating opportunities for individual citizens. These are the only important ends of government. Everything else—defense, environmental protection, taxation, revenue sharing, delivery of health services, criminal justice—all the programs of the bureaucracy are only means to these ends. Merely perfecting the machinery for asset management within the state is not a sufficient end in itself. These assets are meaningless unless they contribute to a better life for people—not just some people but all the people who make the state their home.

This is the inevitable bottom line of government. Are the people of the state better off, healthier, happier, more secure—there are a hundred different yardsticks—than they were before the current administration came to power? The voters keep the box score. Their vote is the ultimate test of success or failure. Unfortunately, there are still too many ways of playing to the grandstand, loading the majority with benefits while keeping the minorities in check, catering to the rapidly growing suburbs while the troubled and troublesome cities are permitted to decay, voting short-term gains at the expense of long-term results.

If the statehouse loses sight of the long-term welfare of all the people, then the "New Federalism" is not going to work. The return of power to the states will have had a brief day in the sun. But before long, we will be back to categorical grants, federal initiative, and restrictive supervision, the loss of local control, and all the ills of big government yet another layer removed from the people.

In the last analysis, it is up to the people. They will get what they are willing to fight for. The ultimate strength of state government is that there is no place to hide. But if the people are too apathetic to go looking, nothing in our democracy will save them.

CHAPTER 4

A Joint Venture

★

For over a generation, it has been fashionable to speak of the public and private sectors of society as if they were totally independent of one another, even antagonistic. Somehow the very words "public" and "private" have developed shades of meaning that perpetuate misunderstanding and fortify distrust.

Thus, simply because it is called "public," one form of television, largely subsidized by foundations and the government and devoid of advertising, is considered somehow more wholesome and socially acceptable than privately owned and operated television—even though the latter is subject to the most rigorous government standards, scrutiny, and control.

"Public ownership" likewise is a label that seems to suggest a dedication of assets to the general welfare, whereas "private ownership" conjures up nightmares of systematic exploitation of the many for the benefit of the few. Faced as we are with the desperately overcrowded agenda of unfinished social business, the emotional distinctions between public and private sectors are no longer relevant—in fact, in many ways the practical differences between them have been rendered meaningless.

After decades of bitter exposure to a variety of restrictive and tyrannical forms of government all over the world, we should know better than to invest the word "public" with any utopian qualities. Public officials—both

Democratic and Republican—have not proven to be any less venal or selfishly motivated than private executives. Public agencies have no more claim to virtue than private institutions. Public education though quantitatively superior in outreach is qualitatively no more effective than its independent counterpart—in many ways substantially less so. Public welfare is no more humanely distributed or beneficial to its recipients than private charity; in some ways, it is even more dehumanizing and degrading.

As social institutions have grown larger and more remote from the individuals they serve, people have developed a numbing sense of powerlessness and alienation. They see themselves as helpless pawns on a chess board dominated by large institutions, especially big government and big business. Caught between them, trapped in a no-man's land between the crushing bureaucracies of public and private sectors, they have developed a myth to ease their anxiety. The myth, repeated so often that it is almost believable, goes like this: since government and business are the major institutions holding and wielding power, and since government represents and serves the mass of people better than business, the power of government should be increased and that of business decreased in order to serve the needs and preserve the freedoms of the individual.

In my experience with government—as a citizen, as a businessman, as a consultant and advisor at the national level, and as a state official, I can affirm that this myth is dangerously false. Leaders of government, like leaders of business, owe their survival to their ability to fulfill the wishes of their constituencies. On the governmental side, irate and dissatisfied voters can oust their elected leaders and thus their appointees from office. On the business side, frustrated and mistreated consumers can force any industry to its economic knees or provoke changes in management through reduced sales and profits.

The problem is that apathy, unresponsiveness, even oppression, do not reside solely at the top—the exposed tip of the institutional iceberg, which can be reached by the vote or the boycott. The real danger to the individual in society lies in the huge concentration of power at the middle level known as the bureaucracy. It is this centralized and monopolistically oriented power that is most dangerous to our social and individual health and has to be minimized at all costs. This is one reason why we have antimonopoly laws to break up bureaucratic concentrations of control. And this is why we must now diffuse political power and thus reduce bureaucracy so that decision-making is centered in that governmental body closest to where the decision will impact and is open to the scrutiny of those most affected.

The real danger to society does not lie in giving power or responsibility to private business as opposed to public government. In fact, there is much evidence to support the opposite contention. The noted psychologist and sociologist Kenneth Clark has said, "Business and industry are our last hope because they are the most realistic elements in our society." Lee Loevinger says, "As between government and business, there are important reasons for leaving as much of the decision-making as possible to business." Peter Drucker has urged the "reprivatization" of many social functions previously undertaken exclusively by government. And even Ralph Nader, cursed in many executive suites as the scourge of industry, insists that strong private business is essential to the social and economic well-being of our society.

When it comes to decision-making that affects the life of the individual citizen, it is far more likely that government will be the monopoly, since business exists with rare exceptions in a highly competitive universe.

Our form of government functions best when its power is least concentrated, and serves most efficiently when it eliminates meaningless distinctions between public and private. This is a political lesson it has taken us a generation to learn. It's also an economic lesson that many businessmen have not yet learned. The social mechanism of a modern industrial society must consist of private and public components meshed together in the common interest, labeled not out of fear or prejudice, but solely because the means of repairing malfunctions differ. If something goes wrong in the public sector, we can vote a governor, mayor, legislator or councilman out of office. If a breakdown occurs in a private institution, we can, as consumers, void the contract, take our complaint to the courts or regulatory agencies, or, through reduced sales, force the private entrepreneur either out of business or to mend his ways. But to assume that the government bureaucrat cares more about us than does his industrial counterpart is dangerous nonsense, especially when that assumption somehow cloaks public institutions in altruism and represents private enterprise as tarred with greed.

Public institutions serving the public interest are qualitatively no different from private institutions serving the public interest. Each is operated by individuals who combine institutional goals with a private agenda of survival and career growth. Each requires effective organization to get its work done. Each must develop the most productive methods of achieving its objectives; taxpayers are as critical of waste and as sensitive to inefficiencies as stockholders. Each must satisfy the demands of its constituency—be they customers or voters—most efficiently and at lowest cost.

In fact, comparing the records of most public bureaucracies with the performance of most successful business organizations seems to give the clear edge to business. Industry over the years has pretty well fulfilled the demands and expectations of society. It has created and distributed a vast array of goods and services, at a cost most could afford, and has produced much of the wealth of the nation out of the abundance of its resources and the labor of its people.

Since 1890, the total real national product has doubled every twenty years. Though population has tripled and taxes have increased sharply, real disposable income per person has more than tripled and hours on the job have declined by a third. Unquestionably, government regulation and "carrot and stick" legislation have played strong roles in this process, but the basic thrust, the organization, and the creative energy have come from business itself.

In comparison, governmental bureaucracies have often seemed to be muscle-bound and short on the fulfillment of their promises. We are all too familiar with schools that don't teach, with a post office system that all but breaks down and has to be "quasi-reprivatized," with welfare programs that have perpetuated dependency for three generations, and with public transportation, which has either disappeared or is in a perpetual state of chaos. All at a "cost" no one can afford.

Business has had its failures, its Edsels and its Penn Centrals, but when it has flopped, it has done so in the glare of public scrutiny. Its ills and errors have been brought to light, and remedies forcefully applied by new management.

With political bureaucracies, however, criticism seems to drive the mistakes ever deeper into obscurity. When a company fails, a more efficient competitor is usually there to take its place. When government fails, the only remedy, after long and anguished soul-searching, is to attempt to pass legislation that will alter or modify the system when only the execution may have been lacking.

Business decisions that are irresponsible, impractical, and unprofitable may be ruinous to the business, but they probably won't cause lasting harm to society. Government decisions, on the other hand, equally irresponsible, impractical, and wasteful, may not touch the bureaucrats who make them, but they can very surely diminish the quality of American life.

Because I do not invest public institutions with any mystical virtues in the execution of public business, I look upon government as a joint venture between public and private interests, and not as a quasi-religious institution established to eradicate private aggression and greed.

Democracy's great strength, especially when coupled with a free economy, is the range of choice available between public and private institutions or combinations of public and private institutions. The Manhattan Project in World War II and the thrust to the moon in the decade of the 60s are examples of the magnificent suppleness of a system which can achieve national objectives through a complex mosaic of public and private activities. In the achievement of any goal, social, scientific, or economic, the choice between "going public" or "private" should be based on potential effectiveness, and not on the label—just as long as the rules of the game are clear and the individual citizen knows who is responsible and what the remedy is if performance breaks down.

Just before he left office, President Eisenhower warned the American people of the dangerous possibilities of collusive monopoly with the military-industrial complex. He was right. A threat to society existed because a monopolistic bureaucracy, clothed in secrecy in the name of national security, created a war machine (and even fought a war) without truly informed consent or citizen participation in the crucial decision-making. The burgeoning of government-operated social welfare programs during the Great Society years led to similar combines in the social arena: the education-industrial complex, the health-industrial complex, and the like.

As long as great national institutional monoliths are constructed to attempt to deal with problems that are essentially local, monopoly will exist, and the people will be dominated by a cold and remote bureaucracy. Only when control of these operations is broken up and localized in the state or community is the threat of bureaucratic monopoly lessened, if not eliminated. There may still be collusion; there may still be influence, but the activity is a lot closer to the people. The locally controlled agency is much more likely to be influenced by business competition and healthy political rivalry than is the huge submerged iceberg of monopoly that federal bureaucracies generally become.

I think the American people are beginning to sort out the relationships between public and private sectors and are starting to understand where their vital interests can be served best. There is a recognizable trend away from abject reliance on federal panaceas. Paralleling this, there is a growing emphasis on local solutions and an increasing demand on business and industry to play a more important role in implementing, if not providing, these solutions.

When a recent Louis Harris poll asked whether business should play a greater or lesser role in social problem-solving, the respondents answered "greater" by a 78–19 percent majority. When asked why they felt this way, they said, ". . . because business gets things done." Broad government promises coupled with blanket national statistics concealed for a long time what the people in the neighborhoods, towns, and states knew all along. Their problems weren't getting solved. Things weren't getting better. National statistics might show 20 percent fewer people living in poverty or 3 percent less unemployment. But the poor knew they weren't getting richer, and the unemployed in the ghetto knew that none of them were getting jobs.

And so the American people are demanding that the resources and the power to decide how they will be used be moved closer to them, closer to where they can be monitored and where the relationship between cause and effect can be perceived directly, not veiled or averaged-out in abstract national statistics.

This I believe is the true genesis of revenue sharing. It is not Republican economics or anti-Great Society politics. It's a response to a felt and expressed need on the part of the citizens to have a greater voice in the expenditure of their tax dollars for programs which are supposed to benefit them. They are acutely aware that somehow the social order in America has gotten out of balance. Greater affluence has not produced the paradise they were conditioned to expect. Instead, it has created a deteriorating environment, a decline in comfort and civility, a reduction in quality of products and services, and a growing distance between the ills of society and those who should be in a position to remedy them.

The people sense that large-scale federal programs have failed. Ten years and more than 200 billion dollars (of their tax dollars) later, there is still poverty, still inadequate housing, still discrimination, still mediocre education, and, recently, a growing awareness of a new and terrifying phenomenon: the drying up of resources and the breaking down of systems whose perpetual supply and effectiveness were once the source of the American dream.

Out of their new perceptions of cause and effect, the American people are looking to their state and local governments for solutions. And out of a conviction that such government cannot do it all, they are rewriting their social contract with that most powerful of all private institutions, American business.

This new contract is the most radical departure yet from our customary perception of the boundaries between public and private. In the past, public institutions have been used to curb the power of private business. Antitrust legislation, the growth of regulatory agencies, tax laws, and similar phenomena have interposed public limitations between the private relationships of business and the marketplace.

But this new contract goes far beyond placing limitations on the actions of business within its accepted sphere of operations. For the first time, it establishes responsibilities for business outside the marketplace, endowing business with many of the powers and obligations once entrusted only to government and holding business accountable for areas of concern once considered solely those of the public sector.

Although all the provisions of the new contract cannot yet be discerned, the nature of the public interest seems clear. Industry is not only held responsible for providing goods and services, but goods that are well-constructed and services whose latent effects are not harmful.

If, in the process of manufacture, industry pollutes the air and fouls the water, industry will be expected to bear the major costs of cleaning the air and water and restoring them to public usefulness. Instead of providing jobs only for those it chooses to employ, industry will be required to provide opportunity and training to social and economic groups traditionally excluded from the job market. And, instead of merely paying taxes for the space it occupies within the geographical limitations of a community, business will be expected to contribute to the social, cultural, physical, and spiritual well-being of that community.

There is a new sense of dissatisfaction with old excuses and outworn systems. The American people are disillusioned with the inefficiencies of government at all levels. They recognize now that their specific local problems are not susceptible to grandiose federal cures. And they sense that business is clearly involved in, if not a root cause of, many of the problems, and therefore must be held responsible for solving them.

Environmental degradation is one of the most obvious of these problems. Industrial emissions and effluents are responsible for the largest amount of both air and water pollution. Federal clean air and clean water legislation has made it possible to establish state environmental standards that local industry, no matter how shortsighted, cannot evade; and these standards have been established on a uniform basis. Environmental degradation has given our states the best opportunity yet to test the developing coalition: government and industry must work together in the public good if we are to have lasting solutions to our social problems.

In Connecticut, industry was capable of making substantial economic sacrifices and creative technological decisions in conforming their operations to air and water quality standards. They did it and are doing it today to the greater good of all, including industry. Faced with a monumental solid waste problem—the generation of ten thousand tons a day with an appalling 50 percent increase predicted by 1985—we were forced to bring social and political theory down to a very practical level: how to win the mundane, but potentially devastating, war against ever-mounting masses of garbage and trash. Here then lies as good an example of a "joint venture" as I know.

The garbage dump may seem an unlikely battleground on which to resolve the discrepancies between political theory and practice. It has, however, many ideal qualities (one of which is *not* that it already smells, as Carroll Hughes, the very able assistant commissioner for public affairs of the Department of Environmental Protection, once suggested). It is far more specific and more immediately threatening than such generalized social areas as health, poverty, and justice. The waves of solid waste never withdraw. Each day each citizen generates an average of 8.6 pounds of it, and he cannot continue to exist if it is not removed. The delivery of health services or of education has been debated for generations. The removal of garbage cannot be debated, as Mayor Lindsay discovered during the 1968 strike of New York sanitation workers. It must be done. If it is not done, the most perfect social system collapses under an avalanche of eggshells, cardboard, beer cans, turkey carcasses, and industrial sludge, to name only the most socially acceptable ingredients of solid waste.

In Connecticut, an industrial state with limited geography and a high density of population, the solid waste problem was immediate and acute. Before we tackled the problem in a systematic way, Connecticut's 169 communities were attempting to dispose of waste as best they could. For two hundred years or more, they simply carted it beyond the confines of town and city and dumped it in the woods. When population growth extended the boundaries of the communities and previously uninhabited land was needed for residential and industrial development, the towns could no longer tolerate random dumping. And so they earmarked certain areas on their periphery as town dumps or trash heaps.

When it became clear that they would soon exhaust the possibilities of these remote areas, a few made investments in the new, but relatively primitive and expensive technology of incineration. They burned what they could, and what was left, they piled up to rot.

Health laws, citizen discomfort, and cost led to the inescapable conclusion that incinerators were not the answer. Growing ecological awareness brought about the condemnation of the town dump and the renaissance of sanitary landfill (a dump kept underground by spreading and covering, at the end of each day, with a legally prescribed layer of earth, usually 6 inches).

Some communities shipped their waste to distant dumping grounds. At one time, the city of Hartford even sold several hundred cubic yards of its garbage to a neighboring community as landfill. (Hartford's then mayor, Dominic DeLucco, achieved passing fame by whispering this fact into the ear of Garry Moore, host of the nationally televised show *I've Got a Secret*.)

Solid waste, however, could not long be kept a secret. Certainly not in the whole of Connecticut. When I took over as commissioner of DEP, virtually all town incinerators were in violation of the new air quality standards. Eighty-nine percent of the state's so-called sanitary landfills were anything but sanitary and were in violation of state regulations, and over 50 percent were found to be polluting surface waters. Like many problems, solid waste transcends local boundaries, but it is too specific, unique, and "localized" for federal solutions.

As with so many other critical areas, the state is the logical vehicle for decision-making and problem-solving. It is small enough to be responsive to local needs, large enough to see beyond purely local interests, and under normal economic conditions has sufficient funds to do the job.

Recognizing the reality of the state's solid waste crisis, the Connecticut General Assembly enacted Public Law 845 in 1971. It made the state responsible for developing a comprehensive solid waste plan to which all cities, towns, and regional authorities would have to conform. The Department of Environment Protection was assigned the task of creating the plan and developing the system.

It could have been a textbook exercise in the temptations of bureaucratic monopoly. The state could have created a new governmental agency, a civil service empire of "trash" which would extend to every corner of Connecticut—a patronage paradise. It could have made local arrangements based on political considerations, attempted a variety of demonstration projects with state and federal money, or wilted like a lettuce leaf in the waste stream under the pressures and temptations of local solid waste lobbyists to delay, compromise, or frustrate the legislative mandate.

Bureaucracy, public or private, has a compelling tendency to reach out to bureaucracy—to join with it to form an ever-larger bureaucracy. We avoided this temptation in Connecticut by finessing all governmental solid waste interests and letting private enterprise compete, not only to develop the most workable plan but to win the construction and service contracts once the plan was accepted.

We enlisted private industry in a public cause, not because it has a monopoly on skills, but because of industry's ability, proven in the competitive marketplace, to solve problems, to produce, to innovate, to manage, and to bring about change. The American people are saying that they want private industry to play a more important role in problem-solving because "they can get the job done." And, in Connecticut, that's what we were interested in.

This is certainly not unique to our free-enterprise system. After all, we have not hesitated to support private enterprise for years, while it devoted its organizational talents to producing instruments of war. Now we must begin to be equally generous in our support while private enterprise helps us to perfect the instruments of peace. To develop a workable solid waste system for Connecticut, one small state, will require a huge capital investment and a pooling of many other talents and institutional capabilities. This joint venture of public and private interests, this new contract for the common good, is another indication of the marble cake texture of American society when it is baked according to its best recipe.

Private enterprise is developing the entire statewide solid waste system in Connecticut. The system must be self-supporting in that the rates charged each municipality for the disposal of garbage and the sale of the recovered materials from this garbage must cover capital and operating costs. As it falls in place over a period of some

fifteen years, the waste disposal system will be administered and financed by a Resources Recovery Authority,
chaired by Malcolm Baldrige, head of Scovill Manufacturing and one of Connecticut's most public-spirited businessmen. Made up of nine private and public members
appointed by the governor and the legislature, the Authority will have the power to raise needed money through
state bond issues and, within certain limitations, to assume
control of privately held lands for their facilities through
condemnation. (The legislation establishing this Authority
carries a unique provision—at no time or under any
circumstances may the Authority have more than 30
employees.)

Even the financing of the initial study stage came from a
"marbleized" mixture of public and private sources, from
the federal and state governments, the state utilities, and
from the General Electric Corporation, the private company which won the study contract.

I selected the General Electric Company from twenty-
two competitive presentations. About half of these were
excellent, and really any of three or four could most
probably have done the job as well, at least based on their
presentations. One thing GE had to commend it was an
understanding of the tricky waters and hidden shoals that
await a private corporation working in the public sphere,
and, *most important,* a willingness to commit itself. Her-
man Weiss, Daniel Fink, Arthur Buecke, Reuben Gutoff,
and Jules Mirabal, the GE management group with whom
I met, fully understood the risks, the uncertainties, and the
political "bait," as well as the potentially limited reward in
these uncharted waters. Yet they still committed themselves. It is to their everlasting credit, and to the credit of
GE, that they moved ahead in a manner that served the
state and its citizens so well.

Since waste originates in local homes and industries, the
state cannot plan or administer an effective disposal

program without the cooperation and support of those political subdivisions and private organizations closest to the source of the problem. Existing municipal systems cannot be ignored since they represent significant local investments. They must be meshed into the system where possible, or phased out on a rational basis where incompatible. Municipal officials and regional planning agencies must be continually involved, as their long-range social and economic planning must dovetail with the planned capacity of the system. And the political argument of "local control over local problems" must be met with a true state-local partnership, or nothing ever begins.

Like all innovative ventures, the Connecticut solid waste plan contains large elements of risk. There have been outcries from those who believe that no private enterprise should be permitted to profit from activities in the public sector. And there have been equal and opposite protests from those unreconstructed businessmen who feel that any governmental involvement in private industry is the socialist camel's nose in the tent of private enterprise.

But, like the separation of powers, the division of risk is also a vital element of our system of government. Concentration of power results either in a reluctance to take risk or, what is more destructive, in a covering up of failure. Division of risk and the pursuit of common objectives expose each participant to the possibility of failure, but assure cooperation and, at the very least, understanding in the event of failure. More important, they create a far better environment for success in the long run.

If the enterprise is successful, if the "marble cake" bakes properly, everyone wins. In the case of solid waste, the federal government wins because it will have at least one effective answer to an acute national problem; Connecticut will have served, in the words of Justice Brandeis, as "a laboratory for a novel social and economic experiment." Connecticut wins because it will have a practical solution to its involved solid waste disposal problem. The communities win because they will be rid of their garbage with a potential profit from resource recovery. The private company wins because it will be able to profit from its execution of the "contract" in all its forms. And the people win because the environment will be cleaned at low cost, and, as a by-product of the system, finite materials will be recovered, and a low-cost energy source, through recovery of combustibles in garbage, will be created.

In addition, everyone wins because the free-enterprise system is reinforced at a time when victories are few and far between.

Just as advocates of government control resist the entry of private enterprise into the field of public service, many businessmen are totally opposed to activities which place business in combination with government and usually require some form of governmental restriction and/or regulation. They see the alliance as an effort to cripple free enterprise, just as their ideological opponents view it as an attempt to subvert government.

Both, of course, are wrong. And, as usual, the majority of the people at the center are far ahead of both extremes. A Louis Harris poll recently asked a cross section of citizens whether business should help solve public problems in the future. A substantial majority said yes. And the higher the income and the educational level of the respondents, the more strongly they believed in this principle.

Significantly, the greatest number felt that business should be a partner of government at the local level, and a substantial majority advocated business involvement at the state level. But at the federal level, where there is the greatest risk of bureaucratic collusion and hidden manipulation, there was far less certainty that business and government should be partners. In fact, a substantial majority felt that business should not be engaged at all in governmental problem-solving on the federal level.

Thus it seems apparent that the public is looking to hometown and home state industry to engage increasingly in private resource and revenue sharing—where it is out in the open and relatively easy to control.

Before I entered state service, I had been exposed to the myth that every statehouse was controlled by business interests. Experience has taught me that this is far from the case. One of my great criticisms of the public-private contract in the state's civic business is the inability of the private sector to convey its message. Business is not the ogre that controls the design and execution of government policy from smoke-filled rooms and behind closed doors. In fact, I found that business has great difficulty presenting its case, even when it is clearly valid. Business, I have concluded, is the stepchild of the statehouse, not its favorite son.

For this, both are at fault. One day when I was visiting one of Connecticut's most progressive and community-minded banks, the Director of Community Relations gave me a briefcase imprinted with the bank's logo. "You can carry it inwards," she told me, "so the seal won't show"—I told her I would be proud to carry it face out.

Traditionally, there is a knee-jerk reaction on the part of business when government seeks to regulate any of its activities. When we first announced the general outlines of our Clean Air Plan for Connecticut, the state's businesses reacted with great alarm and sent up dire threats of mass plant closings and an exodus of industry to more favorable locations. While these pronouncements made a flurry of headlines, they were as ritualistic as a Japanese tea ceremony. We have become so accustomed to thinking of

the public and private sectors as adversaries that we react
with instinctive suspicion when we are asked to treat them
as partners, or even to deal with them as equals.

Because of this climate of mutual suspicion, the state's
approach to cooperation with business could not be simple
and direct, but as oblique as the mating dance of the
ruffed grouse. With the Clean Air Plan, I had to assume
the burden of proof, defining our objectives, indicating
their necessity, and spelling out the federal laws under
which we were operating. At the same time, I had to
demonstrate our good intentions towards those companies
for whom compliance would impose burdens and suggest
possible areas of compromise or change.

Once we moved into an area of understanding, I found
that business was quick to recognize the possibilities of
self-interest as well as community interest in a significant
area of social responsibility. When we developed the entire
mosaic, most businessmen agreed that they must not
continue dumping emissions and effluents into air and
water. What they did ask, though, was to be treated fairly,
with understanding and not blame. They wanted assur-
ance that they would not be put at a disadvantage in
relation to competitors from other states. They wanted to
know that the laws would be administered equitably. They
wanted assurances that we had some understanding of the
problems of the marketplace and the competitive difficulties of operating at a profit. They wanted proof that we
were not simply make-work bureaucrats, imposing regulations because that's what we got paid for. The government
officials who took part in the clean air discussions had to
be convinced, in turn, that the businessmen were not just
selfish profiteers seeking to circumvent the laws for the
benefit of their own pocketbooks.

After several weeks of give and take with industry, we
had developed a much better and more workable clean air

program for the state. Beyond that, we had a set of regulations in whose design and development private enterprise played an essential and important role. It was not the bureaucrats' law being imposed on business, but a joint set of standards, tough, but not unfair or unrealistic, which would be adhered to because it was theirs as well as ours.

Admittedly, it was easier to produce understanding and come to a meeting of minds because I had been in business—had, as the cliché goes, "met a payroll" from day one of a company I had helped establish. I do not underestimate the importance to the working of our system of maintaining a constant flow of "payroll meeters" to the ranks of the bureaucracy—people who speak the language and understand the objectives of the "payroll meeters" sitting on the other side of the governmental desk.

Because much of government is asset management, there is a good argument for salting the bureaucracy with businessmen. Not third-echelon discards whom business is happy to lose to civil service, but key management people whom business could not afford to lose, even temporarily, except for a larger good.

While existing programs of part-time volunteer services and paid leaves of absence are worthwhile, not enough of them are in existence. Even if other enlightened business firms provide pools of employee talent on the same basis as IBM and Xerox, the total will be too small ever to achieve critical mass.

The need is so great that an annual cadre of one or two hundred loaned executives can be absorbed without a trace by understaffed, overworked social agencies and governmental units. As Governor Wendell Anderson of Minnesota has said, "I feel that every government structure in the country should make better use of private business brains for advice. These men in private business have to be efficient, or they go broke. It's only logical to have them pass on their know-how to government." [22]

Based on this philosophy, Governor Anderson invited his state's corporations to involve their leadership in an extensive study of state government, together with recommendations for its improvement. "It's easy to sit around and criticize from the sidelines," he said, "but if you think our state's government is so inefficient and wasteful, come in here and show us exactly where and how we can make it better." [23]

The results, according to all reports, were spectacular. In a six-month period, more than one hundred volunteers from dozens of Minnesota companies gave a total of twenty-six man-years to a study of government. They came up with 138 recommendations that will, if put into effect, save the state more than $75,000,000 a year and improve the efficiency of state services, even while major savings are being accomplished.

In Connecticut, Ted Etherington, former president of the American Stock Exchange and Wesleyan University, headed a similar commission with equally impressive results. As an indication of the significance the new administration placed on this commission, it was created under Executive Order #1. The fifty-nine commission members, all serving full time on leave from their regular assignments, were divided into five teams which met for three months. At the end of this time, they issued a three-hundred-page report which contained 821 recommendations involving savings of $130 million annually, much of which is now in effect.

This kind of program is extremely valuable, but I doubt if it can be extended over a longer period of time, or even if it can be duplicated once its immediate objectives have been met and the initial group disbands. Some system of regular corporate sabbaticals, through which capable executives can be integrated into state government, is necessary to guarantee continuity and to provide a term of service long enough to be useful to the state, as well as to the individual and his company.

In considering a range of possibilities, I have outlined a plan involving industry and state government which seems to me minimal in scope, but a necessary first step in making state government a true joint venture on a continuing basis.

First, I have proposed that the top five hundred corporations in the United States establish a policy of underwriting the services to state government of one senior executive per year in each state in which they have a significant facility. If on the average each corporation had a significant facility in ten states, this would provide five thousand senior personnel per year to augment the agencies and bureaus of state government. In addition, I would hope that hundreds of local and regional companies with only one or two major locations would follow the lead of the top five hundred and establish a similar program resulting in thousands of additional personnel.

Under the plan, the corporation would pick up the incremental difference in salary between corporate and state paychecks. The state, either through its own funds or through foundations or private donations, would pay its regular salary scale to the executive. If the differential averaged twenty thousand dollars per executive, each corporation would have a two-hundred-thousand-dollar pretax annual investment. This compares favorably with the five hundred thousand dollars that IBM and Xerox estimate their leave-of-absence program will cost per year. For most of the top five hundred, this would constitute a relatively minor after-tax expense, but the return on the investment would, in my estimation, be incalculable.

Second, I have proposed that this program be limited to state service, not federal internships and not private or public nonprofit organizations. Since the state is becoming increasingly the focal point of "active" public policy and administrative action, this is where the cadre of business support belongs. With revenue sharing a reality, the states will be initiating and administering far more programs than their already overburdened supply of manpower can handle. An infusion of executive talent from business and industry will do much not only to deflate the myth of hostility between public and private sectors but to correct the ignorance and misunderstanding that presently exists between government and business. Just as important, a much needed and rapidly growing job will get done better through the services of the best of private industry's talent.

While I do not seek to erase all distinctions between public and private, I believe that those differences perpetuated out of fear and distrust are hurtful to society. By making the state a laboratory for corporate executives, we will not only provide skilled public servants but we will begin to bridge the knowledge and experience gap that yawns between corporations and the states in which they are located and do business. Why should there be mindless and robotlike opposition each time state government proposes new taxes or environmental regulations? And why, on the other hand, should legislators and bureaucrats go through the destructive exercise of proposing laws and ordinances clearly discriminatory, confiscatory, or totally insensitive to the justifiable needs of business?

After their year in state government, these executives would return to their jobs with a new dimension of experience and a new ease and familiarity with the legislature, the statehouse, and the bureaucracy, whose influence on their corporate growth can be so critical.

Just as important, the executive and legislative branches of government would have a far better understanding of the needs and objectives of those business organizations, which, after all, are job-supplying and tax-providing citizens of their state.

Third, I have proposed that an Institute for State Government be created jointly by the states, foundations, and corporations involved in the executive sabbatical program. This Institute would conduct research and make recommendations for the improvement of state government based on the collective experience of the corporate executives who have served in the program. It is ridiculous that significant studies, like those produced by Minnesota's Volunteer Loaned Executive Action Program and Connecticut's Etherington Commission, should be limited to a single state at a single time when they undoubtedly are applicable at least in part to the problems of all states. The Institute would serve as the clearing house for such findings and the initiator of additional studies at the request of state officials. Functioning like the Brookings Institution at the federal level, the Institute would be available to assist each of the states in the solution of its most compelling administrative problems from the direct-line experience of men and women who have worked there.

Such public-private collaboration is indispensable to the success of state government. In my experience, most of the people running the business functions of the state have not had adequate exposure to the techniques of modern business management. Even though state salaries are slowly becoming more competitive, the able, young staff member is constantly being tempted by offers from private industry which the state cannot match. A regular infusion of corporate executives would not only upgrade the technical administrative skills of state government but might also create pressures whose inevitable result would be a greater equalization of salary scales. This has already happened on the federal level. With power and importance shifting to the states, it must happen there too.

I am convinced that firsthand knowledge of the workings of state government is indispensable to good corporate citizenship. The concept of society as a partnership
—a joint venture between the public and the private—is
no longer a pious platitude or the excuse for backroom
collusion. It is becoming a working reality, especially at
the state level where most of the gut problems are located
and where most of the solutions are going to take place.

In muckraking books like *America, Inc.* and others of
Ralph Nader origin, the public is being told that the
wealth and resources of America are being funnelled into
corporate treasuries by an unholy alliance of big government and big business. In his introduction to *America,
Inc.*, Nader says, "So much of government authority is
utilized to transfer public wealth into corporate coffers
that Washington can be fairly described as a bustling
bazaar of accounts receivable for industry-commerce." [24]

While such generalized condemnations are in themselves suspect, we have had ample evidence in recent years
of the devastating and debilitating impact of a few public
and private bureaucratic combines. The refocusing of
attention and reallocation of resources to the state are
evidence that these glacial powers are being broken up.

In most of our states, the power and wealth of industry
are fractionated. Competition, and not collusion, prevails.
Because of advances in communication and transportation technology, many more states can provide attractive
locations for almost any kind of business except, perhaps,
to those extractive industries which must be located at the
source of supply. Statehouse domination by a single
interest is becoming the rare exception. Even when it is
present in theory, the growing sophistication of citizens,
the scrutiny of the press, and the increased aggressiveness
of the courts rarely let it take root. It is in the interest of
business to make certain that although it cannot control
(and it should not control), it should lend its unique

resources to creating the most favorable political and social environment in which to live and prosper.

This is what the people are demanding as they recoil from the revelations of secret deals and misused political power at the national level. In the states, such unethical relations between corporate and political bigness would be more difficult to carry off. There is no place to hide, and inevitably, where there is conflict of interest or improper influence, its geographical proximity to constant and immediate inspection quickly root it out.

From what I have observed, most businessmen want to do what is best for society on the state level because it is here that society is not a generalization, but industry's own backyard. What industry cannot tolerate is a climate of bureaucratic indifference, administrative confusion, fiscal irresponsibility, and political expediency. The presence of these flaws over the years has created industry's disrespect for state government, just as single-minded pursuit of profits, regardless of social results, has created deep antagonisms towards business on the part of government and the people. With a large direct contribution from business leadership, these are precisely the areas of state government most susceptible to improvement. With true cooperation under the watchful eye of the voter, the legislator, and the local official, public and private sectors on the state level can more effectively undertake the crucial joint venture of making our troubled and problem-ridden society work.

CHAPTER 5

Budget Is Policy:
Financing—
What, Where, and How

★

There is no better place from which to view the elaborate ritual of state financing than the commissioner's seat in a state agency. After ten years of managing a business that managed other people's money, I thought I knew something about money management and fiscal affairs. But I discovered that running a business is a relatively straightforward proposition compared with the financial convolutions of state government. And the lesson was painful.

In business, the ultimate measurement of success, when everything else is factored out, is that intractable set of numbers on the bottom line. They have to stand up to hard, searching questions, if not by would-be analysts, at least by management itself. Are the earnings solid, or are they the product of bookkeeping sleight of hand? Have profits met forecasts? Do they represent one-shot windfalls, or are prospects good for continued product development and corporate growth? Are earnings generated internally through sound management and successful marketing, or do they only represent assets added through merger or acquisition?

Above all, businessmen must meet the ultimate test. Does it look as if they can and should survive? Is cash flow (noncash charges, like depreciation, plus profit) enough to meet operating expenses and pay the current portions of company debt? If there is doubt, management must react swiftly and successfully, or the enterprise will die. The penalties for this failure are greater than cynics know. The leaders of a bankrupt company lose not only their jobs and money but their respect as well. And it is almost impossible for them to raise new funds and start again.

Most businessmen evidently feel that politicians should be subject to the same kind of scrutiny, the same kind of test. This is why they are the most vociferous complainers against waste, mismanagement, deficit spending, and other unbusinesslike practices they attribute to public administration.

Government, however, is not business, and the bottom line is not earnings per share. The function of government is to satisfy the real or imagined needs of a majority of the people—retaining enough power to stay in office while distributing enough to keep the opposition satisfied. Politics has been called the art of the possible; sometimes public awareness broadens what is possible, and the barriers to progress fall. But more typically politicians give the people what they want before attempting to furnish what they need. And the will of the people is mercurial, to say the least. There are periods when they demand tight fiscal controls, and others when they don't seem to care how much is being spent so long as the impact on them is not too severe. While professing a love for independence and freedom, they want government to pay for an ever-increasing list of services designated as public. But woe betide the elected officials who try to extract the payment without alleviating the pain (or even to extract payment *with* alleviating the pain). The majority of the voters seem to prefer sales taxes that nibble at their assets to income taxes that take larger, more obvious bites. As long as the operation is performed under anesthesia, they usually don't react. But when the knife begins to hurt, the surgeon had better watch out. And always in the background is the comforting delusion that "someone else" is paying. Alas, as Barry Commoner points out in his excellent book, *The Closing Circle*, referring to environmental problems, "There is no such thing as a free lunch." In the end, we all pay for what we get.

As former Governor John Chaffee of Rhode Island can attest, otherwise popular governors who have tried to impose a state income tax often find themselves rejected at the end of their term, while governors whose state deficits are astronomical oftentimes find themselves swept back into office again and again.

A business that operates at a loss cannot long endure. A political subdivision that tries to balance its budget is not so certain of success. Cutting services and controlling expenses cause one kind of pain. Imposing taxes to pay for broad benefits causes another. On election day, the measure of political success is not solvency, but whether a majority of voters believes it has obtained the greatest gain with the least pain.

For fiscal year 1973, the state of Connecticut reported a surplus of $70 million, the largest in its history. The governor was not embarrassed by this result, as it represented, for his three years in office, a dramatic turnaround from a deficit almost four times that amount rolled up by the opposition party. To achieve this surplus, the governor had imposed a Draconian austerity on all branches and departments of government. Departmental budget increases were held to a fixed minimum. Moratoriums were placed on hiring and state salary raises, including merit raises. Welfare benefits and qualifications were drastically overhauled. The highest sales tax in the nation was imposed upon the people of Connecticut, which produced far higher revenues than anticipated, while state aid to towns and cities was held level.

For all his superb generalship in the battle of the bottom line, the governor's personal popularity ebbed. The fact that the state had faced a $250 million deficit when he took office and the effort he laboriously devoted to reversing this trend were soon overshadowed by recriminations directed at reduced programs.

But politics is a volatile process. Since, by law, the state surplus has to be applied to the following year's budget, there was ample opportunity to please the voters by lowering some taxes, holding the line on others, and even sweetening the pot with additional grants to towns and cities and salary raises for state civil servants.

Political damage had been done by the very nature of the businesslike priorities established by the governor. For a while, the public seemed content with the contrast "Tough Tommy" Meskill offered to the sunny and generous John Dempsey. But the public is fickle, and as the pain of reduced programs mounted and the press comment became increasingly sharp, the opinion polls reflected a series of sharp declines in the governor's popularity almost in direct proportion to his success in bringing under control the financial affairs of the state.

As the commissioner of a state department with a broad popular and legislative mandate to clean up Connecticut's environment and halt the spread of pollution, I was in a good position to experience at first hand the effects of the governor's fiscal program—especially as his strategy was interpreted and executed by his finance commissioner, Adolf Carlson.

I had been taught that government policy in the form of legislation, and the funds to support policy in the form of appropriations, reside in the legislative branch, while the office of the chief executive officer is to influence policy before the laws are made and to execute it once the laws are signed and on the books.

But in recent years, state and federal budget offices have

brought to government practice that business truism "budget is policy." Increasingly, it is an ironclad budget put together and administered by the Executive, and not legislation and subsequent appropriation, that defines policy. On the federal level, former President Nixon went so far as to impound funds to maintain his budget, even though legislative power and prerogatives may have been thwarted. A case in point is the Federal Water Pollution Control Act Amendments of 1972, the so-called Muskie Bill. While the bill provided $18 billion of total program funds over five years, the administration chose to release only $9 billion. This decision established definitive water pollution control policy and substantially changed the long-term control strategy for every state. And it was done completely outside of the expressly legislated policy of Congress.

This may or may not be sound business, but it is tremendously frustrating to the legislators who pass what they believe are good laws and to the civil servants who attempt in good faith to administer the programs established by these laws. And it can create bitter frustrations in those segments of the public which have pressed successfully for social legislation and expect to share in its benefits.

Successive Connecticut legislatures, riding the crest of environmental concern in an ecology-minded state, have given the Department of Environmental Protection an immense set of responsibilities, especially in the areas of maintenance, inspection, service, compliance, and enforcement. Federal clean air and water standards must be monitored and enforced. Coastal and inland wetlands have to be regulated and protected. An entire statewide solid waste program—where before there was nothing—has to be set in place. Short-staffed, but under the legislative gun, I tried to convince the governor and his finance commissioner that budget is intelligent policy only when it realistically reflects program requirements, not when it sets arbitrary ceilings based on previous departmental allocations, allocations which had nothing in common with current programs except the name.

This was a difficult principle to sell because the governor was determined to hold down spending in every area, and he felt he could not justify giving one department a substantially larger increase than another, even if its statutory responsibility was greater or its mandate broadened.

While the governor gave genuine support to all the legislation needed to protect the environment, his enthusiasm did not extend to making budgetary exceptions for the department. The governor's position was that there was usually so much fat in the state's departmental budgets that all new programs could and should be absorbed out of the excesses of the old. Another and better way to do the job is through the process called "zero budgeting." This, in its simplest form, is the analysis of every program from "zero," not from the level of the previous year. Obviously this is tough because, by definition, every state civil servant has his job tied to some old program. Analyzing his program from zero does not inspire full cooperation, to say the least.

The practice of using the previous year's budget as a base for the following year's appropriation is unrealistic nonsense. Needs and priorities change. A vestigial division or anachronistic function is often perpetuated only because automatic increases are applied across the board. Budgeting by looking backward is not always adequate for future needs. In any given year there might be unique and unusual pressures on welfare, transportation, environment, education, or other state services. True, it's more work to budget from zero each year and it often calls for painful self-examination, sometimes even self-elimination. But zero budgeting reflects far more realistically the true needs of the state, rather than protecting a bureaucrat's domain or a finance commissioner's bookkeeping.

Fighting for more departmental dollars with the governor who appointed you to your job is not the most productive aspect of public service. Under a zero budgeting process the contest is far less frustrating, at least for the commissioner if not for some of his people. Then you can make your case based on a completely up-to-date estimate of need. New responsibilities can be given adequate treatment, unencumbered by either policy or budget related to the past. Too often in state government, budget not only is policy but precedes policy, limits policy, and often frustrates policies for which the people through their elected representatives have expressed their approval.

I fought for the concept of zero budgeting in the state, and the governor bought it. He instructed his finance commissioner to implement it, and in the Department of Environmental Protection, we practiced it. The only missing link was that we couldn't develop programs that required more than a 5 percent "incremental" increase over the previous year, no matter what program requirement might dictate. We found that the finance commissioner's staff couldn't have cared less about the zero budget narrative we patiently expounded. They only wanted to know what the overall yearly incremental increase amounted to.

Dealing with those people nearly drove me crazy. The only way we were able to get by at all was to use every bit of creative energy to qualify for extra federal dollars. And this we did under the able leadership of Douglas Costle, deputy commissioner and later commissioner of DEP. In fiscal 1973, Connecticut received one-third of all Federal Air Control funds from Region I, which includes all the New England states. We received substantial extra Water Control funds and one of five major solid waste grants for all of the fifty states. When Deputy Commissioner Costle

and I weren't fighting with Adolf Carlson and the bureaucrats of Finance and Control, we were massaging the feds.
Clearly, the latter was more productive than the former,
which may demonstrate one profound weakness in state
government—the ability of one single bureaucrat to
thwart the mandate of the people.

Administration of a budget can be geared to broad
objectives or limited by demeaning conformity. All too
often a budget is treated as a bureaucratic straitjacket, not
as an expression of the public will. Rewards and penalties
to administrators are based not so much on the attainment
of objectives as on the means of getting there. There is
little or no program evaluation based on efficient and
effective delivery of service, only on the amount and
timing of the money spent. Operating a budget as if all
dollars were alike is to forget totally the meaning and
source of those dollars. It is this "paper clip" mentality
which short-circuits the efforts of creative people in both
business and government. I believe the public would much
rather see programs work in their behalf than be com-
forted by the knowledge that even though the programs
failed, every dollar was spent as earmarked. Unfortunately, this nuance was lost on the Department of Finance
and Control, and their inflexible administration of the
state's budget was dramatized for me in what became
known in our department as the "twelve-dollar-and-
eighty-cent misunderstanding."

One of our key staff members was asked to attend an
important Tri-State Planning Commission meeting on
solid waste management to be held in New York City.
Because there were some problems involved in finding a
convenient day for all to attend, the final scheduling of the
meeting took place only four days before the event itself.

As soon as he was apprised of place and time, the
department member submitted a travel authorization form
required for all out-of-state travel. The total expense

involved came to twelve dollars and eighty cents. No approval was forthcoming from Finance and Control, and without it, the staff member would not be able to leave the state on official business. Several telephone calls were made. The Department of Finance and Control was adamant: the rule was that all out-of-state travel had to be approved at least five days ahead of schedule. This request missed that deadline by one day.

To solve the twelve-dollar-and-eighty-cent question, several hundred dollars' worth of administrative time was spent soliciting approval, which was finally given on the very morning of the meeting. Budgeting, in this case, was the end, not the means, of fulfilling policy. Because I took as gospel the warning of Commissioner Carlson that any future late submission would "be returned without approval," several hundred dollars more in personnel time were spent to investigate the twelve-dollar-and-eighty-cent misunderstanding.

When all the evidence was in, it was clear that the travel request could not have been submitted five days in advance because the meeting had not yet been scheduled. (It also turned out that the original request that one of our staff members attend the meeting had come from Finance and Control, but fortunately, for my sanity, I didn't know that at the time.) I shipped the complete file, by this time inches thick, to Adolf Carlson with the comment, "With *all* we have to do, don't you think we could spend our time more productively than this?" No answer.

Perhaps this beady-eyed focus on twelve-dollar-and-eighty-cent items had much to do with getting Connecticut's budget under control and sealing the leaks that had led to previous deficits. But I doubt it. Also, the total lack of regard for the *values* represented by the dollars has also, I am certain, contributed to a rigid focus on imagined "problems" at the expense of real "opportunities" to serve the citizens.

The budget is a fair description of the state's priorities as measured against its resources, and it is policy. The administration of the budget represents the spirit in which these priorities are carried out. It can be a spirit of meanness or generosity; breadth of vision or literal-mindedness; generous attention to the needs of all the people or narrow preference for influential voter blocs. In my judgment, there is no area of state government where greater strides can be made than in creative budget administration and review—and where less is presently being done.

Ultimately, any budget, no matter how administered, depends on revenues. And the ultimate source of the state's revenues is the pocketbooks, bank accounts, paychecks, and balance sheets of its private and corporate citizens. These revenues come to the state through an increasingly intricate network of financial channels. Most of these have to do with taxes—income taxes, sales taxes, user taxes, inventory taxes, payroll taxes, excise taxes, and so on. Some revenues are derived from fees, tolls, and tuitions. Thirteen states have legalized lotteries and are promoting them vigorously as a painless means of raising funds for specific purposes.

In addition to the revenues generated in the states, the federal government, through subsidies, categorical grants, grants-in-aid, and, now, revenue-sharing programs, is spreading more than $30 billion among state and local governments and spending directly more than three times that amount within the states.

Never before in history have Americans demanded so many government services as they do today. They have come to expect that state and local government will educate their children, help transport them to their jobs, protect their neighborhoods, provide health care, collect their garbage, preserve their environment, create opportunities and facilities for leisure and recreation, rebuild their cities, create and maintain a stable climate for business and industry, protect them from fraud, and maintain life-support systems for those who are unable to sustain themselves.

But at the same time they are demanding more services, the people are stirring up a tax revolt against paying for what they demand. It seems that after years of deficit spending on the national level, they can't understand why the states can't also operate on a near bankruptcy basis. When a governor dares to put together a creative revenue package which may raise their level of contribution, either the legislature votes it down or the voters reward him, first with a slippage in the opinion surveys and, finally, if he doesn't retrieve his reputation, by defeat at the polls.

On the local level, the public has reacted by voting down bond issues and tax overrides again and again. Between 1958 and 1960, local voters approved 80 percent of all public-school bond issues. A decade later, this figure was down to 44 percent and falling.

It is estimated that by 1980, the amount that will have to be raised by all government to meet public-service demands will be about $600 billion, roughly twice the present level. Eighty-five percent of this will have to be raised from householders who are already clamoring against higher taxes. About three-quarters of the $100-billion increase estimated in state and local revenues over the 1970s will be derived from overall growth in resources and wealth in the nation. The remainder, if it is forthcoming, will have to come from tax rate increases. This means a 15 percent increase in state and local tax rates of all kinds and a 10 percent to 15 percent increase in property tax rates. With cries being raised everywhere that property taxes have reached their outer limit and that state taxes can't be stretched much further, the states are undoubtedly in for stormy times.

Within the state, the problem is greatly complicated by the inequalities that exist between rich and poor communities and between inner cities and suburbs. This is especially applicable to such vital services as education and health, for which local tax channels are too narrow and restrictive to meet the needs and, even in a climate of economic growth, do not expand proportionately to these needs. Moreover, state constitutions drastically limit the methods communities may use to generate revenues.

The property tax, traditionally the tax base established to meet the bulk of local needs, is proving to be an unsound incentive to development. With the burgeoning growth of educational, health, and welfare services demanded at the local level, the clear incentive has been to press for economic development to build the "grand list"—the property comprising the taxable base of a community. Thus, all development is promoted as good, and support is energetically solicited. Lack of planning, however, and lack of understanding of the environmental, social, and community costs of development, both short- and long-term, have often turned this short-term "economic" gain into a long-term quality-of-life loss and, ultimately, economic loss as well. In many instances, there has been no economic gain at all, as the cost of new community services demanded by new development has equaled or exceeded tax revenues generated. If the property tax is to remain at least an important part of the local base, and all indications would seem to point this way, then there must be vastly improved comprehension and planning at the local level to accommodate growth in harmony with environmental and other community needs. In Connecticut, the state is moving, through the Natural Resources Data Bank in the Department of Environmental Protection, under Hugo Thomas, to provide technical consulting services to local communities to assist them in such comprehension and planning.

For more than a generation, city officials have been begging state legislatures for either increased powers to tax on their own behalf or increased financial assistance from the states. Almost without exception, these requests have been denied. State legislatures have been fearful of losing general revenues supportive of programs in the rapidly expanding suburban and rural areas which have traditionally dominated the statehouses. They have also been wary of raising state taxes in support of the cities because of an inherent fear that interstate tax competition might mean a loss of industry to the states which are not making a major commitment to urban programs.

More than twenty years ago, the cities began to get tired of this biennial cold shoulder and petitioned Congress directly for help. The result, as we know now, has been a patchwork of more than a thousand separate programs of subsidies and categorical grants. Most of these are not only insufficient in themselves but require local contributions which can be ill-afforded. Even when they are in place and operating smoothly, many of these programs miss the mark, for the categories of problems they include are not those whose solution is most desperately needed by the cities. And the whole network is laced with the usual bureaucratic overview, review and re-review. Unfortunately, here, there are plenty of places to hide.

As the U.S. Conference of Mayors has reported, "The answer to the plight is simple. Cities need operating money: money to hire police, firemen, and garbage men. Money to build parks and sewage treatment plants. Yet, what the people need in Seattle is not necessarily what is needed in Shreveport or New York or Burns, Oregon. How, then, can Congress design a traditional grant-in-aid program to meet all these needs in the correct proportion for each individual city in America? Clearly, it can't. A completely new approach is needed." [25]

What the U.S. Conference of Mayors has advocated, of course, is a system of unrestricted federal revenue sharing, funneled directly to the cities, based on need and available to local officials to use as they deem best.

But not even revenue sharing at its most effective is going to solve the problems of local communities that don't have the taxing capacity to keep up with the complexity of their needs. While revenue sharing is an important step in restoring the power and responsibility to those governments nearest to the people, the dollars will not be enough to be a panacea even if the formulas are modified to give the cities a larger share.

What the states and their subdivisions need is not a new revenue system which will magnify their differences, but a rational and unemotional approach to taxation that will permit them to work together. Clearly, this is not the case at present. Each level of government is trying to do an adequate job with one fiscal hand tied behind its back. The cities are hobbled by constitutional and statutory restrictions on revenue raising. The states are either using the wrong taxes or applying the correct ones improperly. And the federal government has not yet found the right formula for redistributing funds to the states in the places where they are needed most without reducing the total grant amounts to the cities it has provided in the past.

As I see it, the real problem is the cutthroat competition on the local level to swell the taxable base by sacrificing the basis of a community's real wealth—its land. Because of rising costs of education, welfare, police and fire protection, and other local services, cities, towns, and suburbs have been forced to milk dry their traditional form of revenue raising—the property tax. Despite the usual protests against the property tax—that it is regressive, that it hits hardest at the poor, the elderly, the

retired—I don't believe there is anything inherently wrong
with it. Simply stated, it is a tax against wealth, as opposed
to income. As Mason Gaffney has written, "In America
today to own property at all is to be better off than most.
If one wants to escape the property tax, there is no simpler
route than by being too poor to buy real estate." [26]

What is wrong with the property tax is largely in its
administration which tends to become politicized, favoring
the wealthy at the expense of the poor and assessing large
holdings and corporate property tax at a much lower
percentage of real value than one-family homes. If these
problems and the abuse of political gerrymandering can
be corrected—and they can by state legislation—the
property tax will once again serve its proper purpose: to
raise money at the local level by taxing the most local
source of wealth there is—land and property residing
within the boundaries of the community.

This estimate of the value of the property tax is
supported by research done by the Advisory Commission
on Intergovernmental Relations (ACIR). During a thor-
ough year-long review, the commission found that "despite the unpopularity of the property tax, its real financial
pinch is minimal for the average homeowner—a national
average of 3.4 percent of income out of 20.2 percent for all
taxes." [27]

To protect the poor and the elderly from a disproportionate property tax burden, by January 1974 all 50 states
had enacted some form of property tax relief plans for the
elderly, although only 28 states had done so four years
earlier; these plans, often called "circuit breaker" legislation, cut off the requirement to pay when the property tax
reaches a designated proportion of family income. Like so
many pieces of progressive legislation, the "circuit
breaker" was pioneered in the state of Wisconsin—another testament to the continuous creativity of the states,
in general, and to that state in particular. Recently, in

some states, the concept has been extended to all low income people. Michigan, for instance, has extended its program to both renters and homeowners of all ages.

The major issue, then, is not that the property tax should be repealed, but that its inequities should be eliminated, and much of the burden now imposed upon it should be lifted to the state level. As Commissioner of Environmental Protection, I was appalled by the extent to which the land-use decisions of local communities were dictated by the inadequate local tax structures. This power of taxation ought to be the most effective control we can place on land use. Unfortunately, it is the weakness of taxation, not its power, which is levering most of our present land-use decisions. The Grand List is the primary source of revenue for maintaining the quality of life in our communities. But in town after town, city after city, as the people's demands for services increase they can no longer be supported by an already overburdened real property tax. Overburdened not because it is a bad tax, but because it is usually the *only* local tax permitted under state law and therefore must shoulder the weight of most local expenses.

What is happening in the towns and cities of every state is that the city fathers are literally raping the land—their most priceless asset—to pay the bills. All too often this involves a random, shortsighted conversion of land to commercial, industrial, residential, or other tax-bearing purposes which may very well destroy, beyond redemption, the beauty, character, and environmental balance of the very communities it is intended to serve. And in all too many cases, the new money raised is a net loss because of new services demanded. But unless they bring in large and solvent taxpayers, local governments have to raise tax rates beyond the individual property owner's willingness or ability to pay. When this happens, land and property taxation begin to have a negative effect.

In some cities, the situation has become so acute that property taxes are all but confiscatory. Instead of supporting growth, they are discouraging it. In Newark, for example, buildings are being abandoned so fast that a 9 percent increase in the property tax rate in 1971 resulted in a 3 percent decrease in revenues from that tax.

It is essential, therefore, to remove from the property tax the heaviest local burdens, releasing vital land use decisions from its tyranny and permitting local policies to be made in a more positive atmosphere than the desperation which now characterizes them.

This could be accomplished by requiring that a share of the local property tax be made available on a formula basis to the state—a kind of revenue sharing in reverse. The state, in turn, would add to and redistribute these funds to the communities, primarily to bring their educational expense levels up to the state standard—provided the effort they are putting into education is also up to the state norms.

This kind of revenue sharing would eliminate the inequities in property tax rates that have led to legal actions like the Serrano case in California which has come very close to overthrowing the local property tax as a determinant of eductional expenditure. It would also take the pressure off communities to bring a factory into town simply to increase revenues to meet educational expenses. A factory coming into the state at a more suitable location would have the same effect because a portion of its property taxes would go to the state for general reallocation. As Roy W. Bahl has pointed out, "There is a strong case for transferring the financing of education to the state level. First, the wide disparities in the quality of urban schools and the quality of education available to certain children is at least partially the result of accidents of property tax geography." [28] A Tax Institute of America study confirms this conclusion by comparing the per-pupil assessed valuations between the poorest and wealthiest property tax school districts in Colorado. In 1969, a thirty-eight times greater tax effort was required in the poor district than in the wealthier district to provide an equal dollar level of support. Such an inequitable distinction between rich and poor could be eliminated if the state were more directly involved in evening out local discrepancies in paying for education. The single burden on land for tax revenues would also be alleviated.

Likewise, the other major state expense, welfare, should be removed from both local and state responsibility and made a function of the federal government exclusively. This would take another substantial load from the local and state tax structure and spread welfare costs to all the nation's citizens; not only those who happen to live in a state or city where poverty or unemployment is endemic. A forward step has already been taken in this area. Supplementary Security Income (SSI), a program which went into effect on January 1, 1974, frees the states from a major welfare expense, as the national government now takes over most of the program and administrative costs of aid to the elderly, blind, and disabled.

The case for shifting total responsibility for welfare to the federal government is, I think, a sound one. In the first place, welfare is far less a product of state decision-making than of national policy. In fact, the states themselves have very little control over welfare, especially since the Supreme Court decisions have overturned state residence requirements. Second, the discrepancies that now exist between welfare levels in the various states are not only a clear violation of the spirit of national policy but add to the problems of the cities by encouraging welfare recipients to move from low benefit areas to the already near-bankrupt inner cities where payments are much higher.

Because some state tax systems and/or legislatures are

unresponsive and are not able or willing to grow sufficiently to meet the additional burden of size, nationally determined programs like welfare should be spread to all taxpayers through the medium of the federal income tax which is more responsive and income elastic at the federal level.

There are only two ways that state taxing systems can become responsive, and both have their disadvantages. The first, and most obvious, is an automatic response that is built into the system itself, as in the federal income tax. The second is a discretionary response through periodic rate and base adjustments in state taxes—a process which usually lags behind need, given the slowness of state legislatures and the unpopularity of tinkering with the tax rate.

A state income tax is obviously no panacea, and it has many disadvantages associated with abstract revenue loss or gain, not the least of which is the tendency to build in expenses during good times and then raise taxes to avoid deficits in bad.

More than forty states now have some form of individual tax. Forty-six states have corporate taxes. Between 1942 and 1970, state personal income taxes grew from 2.6 percent to 8.2 percent of all funds raised by state and local governments. During the same period, property taxes declined as a share of state-local revenues from 43.5 percent to 26.5 percent. General taxes, which forty-five states now have, grew from 6.5 percent to 12.3 percent and state corporate income taxes remained at something just under 3 percent.

A recent Harris poll determined that 53 percent of the public believes that "the federal income tax is the fairest way to raise funds." At the state and local level, however, the public clearly prefers a state sales tax (46 percent) with only 32 percent who feel a state income tax is the "fairest". (Notice "fairest," not "preferable." When "preference" is involved, the figures are more skewed toward the sales tax.) Clearly, the administration and the legislature that bite the bullet of the state income tax do so at great political risk (see Appendix, Table 18).

Some states and cities have been seeking an easy way out of the tax bind—the lottery. Connecticut, New Hampshire, New Jersey, New York, and Maryland are all busily in the numbers game, urging their citizens to buy chances, and making some money in the process. Although this may be a painless way to raise money, it tends to come from those who can afford it the least, and as a revenue-raising technique, there are those who feel it creates as many problems as it solves. On the other hand, it is another instance of the states' role as the laboratory of democracy.

Revenue sharing is a significant addition to state and local financial independence and flexibility. But it is not going to provide easy solutions to deeply engrained problems. Certainly, the basis of former President Nixon's "New Federalism," which gave birth to revenue sharing, is totally sound: to bring the capacity for discretionary spending down to those government levels nearest to the people. Categorical grants-in-aid have either by-passed the states completely or created such a thicket of regulations that it has been impossible to see the forest for the trees. Revenue sharing is to be a new way of packaging the hundreds of operating federal grants-in-aid into neater bundles that can be managed, controlled, and understood at the state and local level.

Formally known as the State-Local Fiscal Assistance Act of 1972, the revenue sharing program has an initial five-year life, retroactive to January 1, 1972. Its intent is to return 30.2 billion dollars to the nation's thirty-eight thousand governmental units over the five-year period. As former President Nixon said, "Our ultimate purposes are many: to restore to the states their proper rights and roles in the federal system with a new emphasis on and help for local responsiveness; to provide both the encouragement and the necessary resources for local officials to exercise leadership in solving their own problems; to shift the balance of political power away from Washington and back to the country and the people." [29]

In general, the states may use the funds for any legal expenditure. Local governments, however, are restricted to eight broad areas defined as "high priority expenditures." They are: public safety, environmental protection, transportation, health, recreation, libraries, social services to the poor and the aged, and financial administration.

One major catch, however, lies in the total amounts made available to cities despite revenue sharing. This results from the fact that many of the grant-in-aid programs on which the cities have been relying are either being slashed or phased out of existence. Unless remedial legislation is passed, the net effect of federal grants to the cities will be a cut in urban programs from 4.2 to 2.7 billion dollars; and a reduction of 7 billion dollars in programs for the unemployed, the elderly, the sick, and the young. Moreover, with the cutbacks in or termination of federal model cities, housing, manpower, and allied programs, and the phase-out of funding for the nation's nine hundred and seven Community Action Agencies, it is difficult to see how the cities, at least, are going to come out ahead during the first years of revenue sharing. And, in the long range, the prospect of the program's cutoff in five years could make a lot of cities and states wary of starting programs that depend on revenue sharing funds for their life.

Little wonder that many communities, upon receiving their first revenue sharing checks, decided to put the money into one-shot capital projects, like city halls and libraries, which will not require annual increments that they will be unable to meet. Another unfortunate and unforeseen effect of revenue sharing resulted from the formula for distribution which was based on relative income and tax effort, as well as population. This formula was designed to favor urban and rural areas over the more solvent suburbs, but the first checks indicate that the suburbs will be receiving more than expected and many rural and urban areas will be getting less. What has happened, obviously, is that the suburbs are getting richer from new-found sources of money, while the inner cities are getting poorer from the cutoff in categorical grants-in-aid.

The federal government must establish general policy guidelines in those areas of social services to be administered by the states and cities. But, once the broad policy has been determined, I believe the states and communities should be empowered to make their own spending decisions. I'd much rather have such decisions face the test of the voters resident in the state than depend on the detailed, nit-picking regulations of bureaucrats who live in Chevy Chase or Alexandria. An analysis published in the *National Journal* of HEW categorical grants proves conclusively that categorical grants from the federal government tend to isolate the political structure responsive to the people and strengthen the self-perpetuating bureaucracies spawned and nurtured by Washington.[30] Where there is no authority, there can be no responsibility. Where budget is locked into airtight compartments by the bureaucracy, there can be no true public policy responsive to the will of the people.

Revenue sharing will work only if there is a national determination that the funds will be adequate to the needs, and if the people trust the elected officials at state and local levels to know within a national policy framework what has to be done. Until the recession of 1974, so many states were logging surpluses—$11 billion alone in the first half of 1973–74 compared with $32.4 billion projected federal deficit—there was little excuse for the more acute forms of privation to exist amidst relative plenty. As long as the economy is generally sound and the concept of revenue sharing is supported at the national level, the states and their subdivisions have a golden opportunity to pitch in and solve most, if not all, of the physical, social, and human problems that have been plaguing them. When the economy turns sour, revenue sharing becomes, if anything, more important to the states.

But the shackles should be taken off, and the right to make broad policy-budget decisions should be freely granted. When I fought with Connecticut's Finance and Control Commissioner about the rigidities and stupidities of the state budgeting process, I was really protesting the wastefulness and imprecision of a process that pretends to be controlled and accurate. We were given a budget carefully analyzed by program and specified as to travel, consultants, supplies, and mileage. We knew the price of everything—but no one paid any attention to the value the citizens were receiving. In order to protect next year's budget base (still an incremental budget), bureaucracy fought bureaucracy. It found ways to spend money within categories even when there was no real need to spend it. And it scrimped and starved in other areas where there was real urgency but no additional funds. Bureaucrats don't like to give money back. It's so hard to get in the first place, they'd rather spend it in what they convince themselves is the public good than return it and have it disappear forever into the general fund and impact on the budget of the following year.

I believe there's a larger lesson to be learned. If the states are given relative freedom to spend their revenue sharing allocations, they will develop conscience and muscle, both of which are somewhat flabby from lack of exercise. I believe that local administrators will find better ways of getting the job done than the wasteful, bureau-

cracy-feeding manner which is all they've known for the
past generation. I know that if we had had the freedom to
spend our Department of Environmental Protection
money any way we wanted to in order to attain prescribed
objectives, we would have met our obligations and a good
deal more—faster, better, cheaper, and with much less
frustration.

With a state tax program that provides a sound revenue
base, a state-local property tax to be used to increase
support for and equality in education, a federally funded
welfare system to lift that burden from the backs of the
states and cities, and a creative, efficient state budget
management and review, I believe that the states and their
local communities can begin to address themselves to the
solution of long-standing problems and rid themselves of
the desperate year-to-year search for enough money to
support stop-gap arrangements to keep the whole edifice
from caving in.

Such revenue and management reforms offer the best
program for meeting the rising expectations of the people
as they look to their communities and their states for
increased concern and broadened services. In the words of
Daniel J. Elazar: "Such a combination rests on the
fundamental American premise that the states and localities are the proper and most competent entities for dealing
with domestic problems and seeks to strengthen and
invigorate them as viable partners in the American
Federal system." [31]

That is our goal as concerned state citizens and as
Americans. If state government can rid itself of the
twelve-dollar-and-eighty-cent budget syndrome that continually stultifies its vision and its effectiveness, and if the

federal government can balance its bureaucratic tenden-
cies with a fair regard for its equal partners, the fifty states,
then that goal will be achieved.

CHAPTER 6

Baking the Marble Cake

★

The marble cake metaphor of federal-state relations is an appropriate one. In practice, however, the cake is often half-baked (and, from my Connecticut experience, a few of the bakers are as well). Between the states and the federal bureaucracy, there is an obvious cultural lag. Most bureaucratic thinking has been shaped during the New Deal, Fair Deal, New Frontier, and Great Society eras. Then the prevailing wisdom was nationally oriented. It was felt that the states were backwashes of provincialism and reaction. The "Big Picture" could only be assembled in Washington. State governments could be counted on to be partisan, narrow, selfish, and grasping. The federal presence was necessary to the execution and administration of every program—and why not, they "contributed" all the dough.

In fairness there was and is some justification for this unflattering image of state government. In major confrontations between state practice and national policy, many states have shown a shameful lack of sensitivity to their obligations under the law. This is especially true in areas of rapid social change where it is often easier to call "Charge" from the banks of the Potomac than to advance from the beleaguered chambers of the state capitol.

And so the strong temptation of federal lawmakers and the bureaucrats who write most of the laws is to regard the good intentions of state government with a suspicious squint, and to keep a tight hand on policy guidelines, program administration, and the all important dollar. It is impossible to realize how frustrating and stultifying this can be until you have sat in a state office building eager to solve a problem but constantly faced with the arrogance and nit-picking of an overweening federal presence whose checkbook is bulging when yours is occasionally overdrawn.

This is not to say that the role of national government should be that of absentee landlord or an overgenerous parent who gives his errant son a large allowance without advice, directions, or suggestions as to how it is to be spent. As a state official, I came to respect, even welcome, the role of the federal government as policymaker and standard-setter. It has to be that way. The states are like fifty barges in a narrow, winding channel. Without a tug whose captain has their common destination firmly in mind, the fifty barges are doomed to flounder as they set off in every direction. Even if they have their own outboard motors—taxing power, constitutions, executive and legislative leadership—they probably could not make it alone, and certainly would not be able to get there all together in a united, homogeneous effort.

The federal government must establish direction, create uniform policy, interpret the "chart" (which is the federal Constitution), and make certain that the political, economic, and social goals of the Republic are being pursued equally in every state. It's when the federal crew overruns the barges, takes over the wheelhouse and even tries to design the uniform of the crew, that the situation gets out of hand.

Now, if you wonder how a marble cake turned into a string of barges, let me explain: That's the kind of riddle state officials are confronted with every day as they try to deal with the paradoxes and ambiguities of federal-state relations.

The whole complicated issue was summarized for me in Connecticut's dealings with the Environmental Protection Agency over the clean air and clean water regulations. The former seemed to me a perfect example of the very best mix of ingredients in the marble cake recipe. The latter was an indigestible horror, demonstrating not only that too many cooks spoil the cake, but that too many captains wreck the barge. The contrast is instructive, because it demonstrates far more than abstraction or general principle how well the federal system can work and why so often it goes terribly wrong.

The Federal Air Quality Act was passed in the spring of 1971. Only a short time before, the President had signed the National Environmental Protection Act, setting up a new federal bureaucracy, the Environmental Protection Agency, which was charged with the responsibility of setting federal antipollution policy and standards and overseeing the performance of the states in achieving them.

It is important to recognize the relationship between the newness of the Environmental Protection Agency and its approach to clean air implementation. As a young bureaucracy it had not had time to harden either ideologically or programatically. Like the Office of Economic Opportunity in its salad days, it was staffed by dedicated, eager, young men and women, many of whom had not previously worked for the federal government, but who were attracted by the opportunity to get in on the ground floor of social problem-solving. Unaccustomed to the games federal agencies play, they were, for the most part, idealistic men and women who just wanted to see the environment of America cleansed. As a result, they were willing to establish national air quality regulations and give the states an opportunity to develop their own implementation plans with a minimum of red tape or bureaucratic intervention. It was, it seemed to them, the quickest and most sensible way to get the job done.

In part, the almost casual nature of the charge to the states laid down by the Environmental Protection Agency was due to the uncertain chain of command within the agency itself. No one really knew who had the authority to control state implementation plans, or even how, and so a far greater measure of freedom was accorded than is usually the case in federal grant programs.

In contrast to this, the amendments to the Clean Water Act did not come along until 1972–73, when the EPA was a more mature bureaucracy, whose arteries were beginning to harden and whose staff understood fully such matters as chain of command and bureaucratic prerogatives. EPA now was unwilling to delegate too much freedom, especially to the "suspect" states.

Another reason for the difference between the Acts, and their approach to compliance, was the contrast in air and water quality machinery already in place when the laws were passed. Air pollution control had traditionally been under the thumb of state health departments which regarded air pollution as a problem subordinate to their primary charge and were lax in administering and enforcing state and local statutes, if any. Air pollution control was a stepchild.

Generally, air pollution control, like air pollution itself, is an individual matter. Households, businesses, or industries emit pollution into the air and are, or should be, responsible for cleaning it up. Because water quality, on the other hand, involves massive public works projects like primary, secondary and advanced (or tertiary) sewage treatment plants, there has been historically an entrenched water quality infrastructure in place throughout America. This sewage and public works establishment is made up of people specifically trained in their various technical fields. They have their own long-standing professional associations which are used to dealing with rigorous federal controls and complex legal structures needed because of the huge sums of money involved in water purification.

In contrast, when the Clean Air Act was passed, there was no history of litigation and compliance activity and certainly none of large-scale public works projects. There was no existing technical or legal fraternity. Unlike water quality that had a bureaucratic history, most recently extending back to the Clean Water Act of 1965, the air program started almost from scratch with little or no legislative or judicial history to weigh it down.

Although some of these factors may explain the difference in approach that a single federal agency took to two major facets of the pollution problem, they do not 'change the fundamental principle that one was the right way and the other the wrong way for Washington to deal with the fifty sovereign states.

The Clean Air Act, as originally passed, was in many ways a model of clarity. It gave certain responsibilities to the states and another cluster of responsibilities to the federal government. It recognized the differences in national and state roles and powers, and said in effect, *"Vive la différence."* The federal government's responsibilities were primarily, though not exclusively, to set up national air quality standards that the states would have to meet, together with timetables as to when compliance would have to be achieved. The standards were given in terms of the concentrates of six major pollutants in the air. The Act itself did not say specifically what these standards should be. But the Act did give EPA a mandate to do the appropriate research, look at the economic, social and environmental aspects of air pollution, and decide what primary levels of major pollutant control should be reached by July 1975, and what secondary standards should be reached eighteen months later.

"Elementary," one might say. "Isn't this the way all our laws work?" "No," groans the anguished state official contemplating a stack of water quality compliance paper that rises literally to the ceiling, "It is not." The permissive nature of federal air quality "guidelines" is the joyous exception. It is so clear and rational as to appear almost obscene to those who think that federal intervention should not be like a bikini covering only the vital parts but like a wet suit smothering the entire body politic.

With both reason and humility, the Clean Air Act and its implementation took into account the differences in meteorological, industrial, social, and economic conditions between the states and recognized implicitly that the states had not only the right but the only capability to decide which of many strategies would work best to achieve national standards for each type of pollutant within their specific frame.

As a result, the Act set up a simple mechanism of state implementation planning. Each state was given time to draw up its own plan, submit it to the EPA, which either gave approval or sent it back to the drawing boards because of basic technical failings to meet primary and/or secondary standards. Great freedom was given each state to determine which implementation plan would work best for it. The states were also given some freedom in determining schedules. They could move very quickly, as soon as their regulations were approved and in force, or they could delay—for good reason—so long as they eventually met the primary standards by mid-1975. They could, if they wanted, establish standards of their own even more stringent than the federal government's. They could set their own laws regulating sulfur content of fuel oil, for example, or impose transportation controls, or legislate against certain types of industry if these seemed to be the strategies most likely to meet the national objectives. They had the option to set up "nondegradation" regions, which simply set higher standards on a regional rather than a state basis, if this made sense for their particular state. Remember, however, the minimum objectives were the same for every state; only the strategy in achieving these objectives would vary.

California, for example, with its high levels of photochemical smog, and its geography, was forced to incorporate in its plan a strategy for stringent transportation control. Connecticut, on the other hand, while it may in the future need to adopt such a strategy, could meet the existing federal standards simply by imposing regulations on "stationary" sources such as factories and power plants.

There was a great deal of flexibility permitted all along the line, and I felt that the EPA was going a long way toward expressing confidence in the ability and desire of the states to work out effectively their own air quality programs.

As a result of the independence and creativity allowed under the law, we in Connecticut never felt harassed or put upon by the Feds. We felt that the regional EPA administrator, John McGlennon, was a genuine friend who understood us and sympathized with our problems. Because of this permissive climate we were able to attract to state service a group of extraordinary young environmentalists, mostly volunteers, who helped put together a plan that was at the same time idealistic and workable.

After a series of public workshops and formal hearings throughout the state in which every interest had its input, Connecticut's Clean Air Plan was approved in record time. As a matter of fact, it was one of only nine (and the only highly industrialized state's in the nation) to be permitted implementation of its own air quality program on its original submission without change.

Opponents of strong state government will be quick to point to the many slippages both in schedule and in program content which have occurred since the national clean air legislation was passed. And it is true that some states have taken advantage of federal flexibility to drag their feet, perhaps even to defy the law. But this does not contradict my belief that the ideal federal-state relationship is exemplified by the philosophy and the procedures of the Air Quality Act. If a state is unable or unwilling to comply with federal standards, it is the duty of the federal government to intervene through a system of penalties, disincentives, and remote controls. Just as in the area of civil rights no governor should be able to defy the federal law by barring the door of the schoolhouse, so no state should be able to evade federal environmental policy by keeping its chimneys and smokestacks wide open.

The EPA's attitude toward Connecticut's preparation and implementation of its clean air plan not only enlarged my respect for the federal bureaucracy, but also permitted our aggressive young staff of new state civil servants to respect itself. And even more important, because of the flexibility of approach permitted to us, we were able to review the ideas and suggestions of many important segments of the state's population: individual citizens, industrial groups, environmentalists, and members of the state bureaucracy.

The Federal Air Quality Act permits management by exception which to me is the most effective administrative method for any enterprise. Because the law did not attempt to cross every T and dot every I, it gave us a range of creative freedom beneath that single ironclad mandate —get the job done. If the EPA had tried to legislate every approach to compliance, I believe we would still be arguing with our federal counterparts and bouncing a technologically and politically unacceptable plan back and forth between Hartford and the regional EPA office in Boston—with the citizen the loser.

Now let's look at the other side of the environmental coin—water. Connecticut's implementation of the 1972 amendments to the Clean Water Act is another and much sadder episode in intergovernmental relations, the kind of bureaucratic horror story that fills every civil servant's diary and his notes for the exposé of the red tape jungle he will never write.

In the first place, the Clean Water Act, as interpreted by the Environmental Protection Agency (EPA), does not say to the state, "Take a look at your whole water system and come up with a plan which we will approve if it allows you to achieve new national standards." Admittedly, it would be more difficult to take this approach with water than it was with air. In air pollution it was possible to determine that a few pollutants, six by number, were guilty of creating most air pollution.

In the case of water, however, almost everything we put into it is a potential or actual pollutant. For centuries we've been treating our water courses like sewers, dumping into them everything that will dissolve, float away, or sink. Once out of sight, it has been out of mind. So the federal government felt it was unable to say to the states "Provide us with water implementation plans that will achieve certain standards." It's also likely that by 1972 EPA was unwilling to give the states the freedom even if it believed the states could do the job. As a mature bureaucracy it was unable psychologically to give to the

states the measure of creativity which its youthful counterpart had willingly provided. And so the EPA went to a
"national permit system," a typical bowl of bureaucratic
alphabet soup, the NPDES (National Pollutant Discharge
Elimination System)—which the states may administer
through their own agencies, but only when a mile-long
laundry list of precise standards, techniques, measure-
ments, inspections, and penalties has been approved first
by the federal regional office.

In other words, instead of establishing broad policy and
letting the states come up with locally workable solutions,
the federal government produced the details of implementation and instructed the states to administer them
through absolute adherence, not through independent
planning. Instead of being master in its own house, as with
the air quality program, each state was made an inden-
tured servant of the federal government in executing its
water program. What applied to Connecticut also applied
to New Mexico, only the difference was a lot greater than
the distance.

As a further complication, there were differences of
opinion between the regional and national EPA offices.
This showed up first in Connecticut's "permitting" request. In order to qualify for permanent authority to issue
our own discharge permits based on federal detailed
standards, we needed to make statutory changes in our
laws and procedures. After extensive negotiations with our
good friends in Boston we received their approval. Then,
we helped the state legislature's Environmental Committee
draw up a bill implementing these changes. It passed the
General Assembly and was signed by the governor. The
regional EPA then checked with Washington and was told
"No, we want a few changes." By this time, it was too late
to go back to the legislature, which was going out of
session, so we were forced to adopt a series of patchwork
administrative directives to fill in the supposed holes,

probably extralegally. Aside from the embarrassment, it was an administrative zoo.

The new water law provided that local industries must pay their pro-rata share of the cost and operation of sewage treatment facilities to which they contributed wastes. Fair enough. To implement this provision, the state had to come up with a detailed plan by March 31, 1973, indicating how local industries would be charged. By March 31st, the federal EPA had not yet forwarded the new federal guidelines to the state so that the municipalities could develop their plans. But, at the same time, the municipalities were not allowed to get federal grants unless they had such plans—and the waters remained polluted.

This ridiculous circumstance is the administrative opposite of management by exception. The young enthusiasts of the early EPA were willing to sacrifice federal control to get results, so they put faith in the states' ability to achieve them, yet monitoring output. By the time they had become middle-aged bureaucrats—and bureaucrats age rapidly—they were haggling over every word, line and paragraph and losing the forest for the trees. Granted, many states might not have acted as rapidly and energetically as Connecticut to conform to federal environmental laws. But then, as in every other area of federal policy, the government has a powerful arsenal of sanctions to impose, such as the withdrawal of independent privileges or the withholding of further funds.

Unfortunately, however, the federal government is often more interested in legalistic niceties than in actual performance as a measurement of success (and here they're similar to the state's budgeting process). Under air quality legislation only the end result was what mattered—the detailed milestones were relatively insignificant. With the Water Quality Act, the ultimate goal seemed less important than a whole succession of "Checkpoint Charlies" bristling with machine guns and calculated less to let the states go through than to harass them and complicate their journey.

Only when individuals or institutions face each other as adversaries, it seems to me, should the emphasis be on barriers rather than on access. Canada and the United States have three thousand miles of common border with only a handful of customs posts to impede crossing, and these are largely for mutual benefit. On the other hand, the access to East Germany on the Autobahn is studded with checkpoints and delay stations. Under air quality regulations, the federal government established a destination, handed the state a map of the territory and said, "Okay, tell us how you want to get there." Under the Water Quality Act, they marked out the precise route and said, "If you satisfy us that you can meet our conditions, we'll let you man the checkpoints." This is scarcely a creative approach to building initiative and/or capability in the states, an objective which should be one of the most important in all federal-state relationships.

All these water compliance requirements resulted in a mountain of paperwork which Bob Taylor, the hard-working, dedicated head of DEP's Water Compliance, estimated at one point would literally reach the ceiling of our State Office Building if piled in one stack. (Our offices at the State Office Building had monumentally high ceilings.) More important, these federal requirements were taking an estimated one-third of his time, and contributing nothing to getting his job done.

Indeed, I estimate that at least 50 percent of the time of the staff of our Water Compliance Unit was spent answering questions from EPA, both regional and Washington based, about our program, rather than achieving the reductions in pollution the overall program was supposed to bring about.

Yet there is hope for Congressional realization of the need for change. Hearings began in the spring of 1974 on a major part of the Clean Water Program—the emergency plan to help communities in building waste water treatment plants. The conclusion of these hearings is best illustrated by Congressman Jim Wright of Texas, chairman of the Investigations and Review Subcommittee of the House Public Works Committee as he summarized the hearings:

"Cut to less than half its intended size by a series of arbitrary executive impoundments, the program has been further emasculated by an almost unbelievable proliferation of administrative red tape.

"Incredible though it may seem, the administration has managed to construct a fantastic maze of baffling guidelines, burgeoning regulations, bewildering paperwork and ever-changing directives which have brought what was an ongoing program to a virtual halt."

Every functionary on every level of government has his own favorite horror story of red tape and bureaucratic obstructionism. This saga of water quality standards is mine. Yet, when all the reports are in and the last footnote on the last page has been translated into computer symbols, the federal government is going to have to rely on the states to administer the plan and enforce the standards—in short, to achieve results.

At the end of the long paper chase, Connecticut was granted the right to grant its own permits, but still with horrendous bureaucratic restrictions. But how could it have ended up any differently? With something over three thousand point sources of water pollution in this small state alone, it would have been impossible for the federal government to move in troops of inspectors to do the job. And even if the manpower were available, the cost would have been prohibitive.

This kind of federal approach ultimately discourages many states from becoming independent or bothering to staff themselves to handle difficult responsibilities (ignoring the difficulty of attracting dedicated staff under such circumstances). While Connecticut, with its native pride and traditional independence, was first in New England to begin to slay the red tape monster, many other states in the region are now telling EPA, "We don't want to be bothered. You want the water cleaned? Then *you* see that it's done." And then the Feds will say, "Okay. If you don't want to conform, you'll lose money." The withholding of federal funds will mean a further loss of manpower and a greater paralysis in the state's inspection and enforcement machinery. And inevitably this will result in no movement and in dirtier water.

Negative feedback of this kind all too often interferes with effective interaction between the various levels of government. The solution? Begin to treat the states as equal, friendly powers with the ability to meet national standards and execute national policy. Crack down if the states refuse to comply with federal standards whether in racial equality, land use planning, public education, welfare, or water pollution standards. It is not up to the federal establishment to tell the states *how* they must execute the policy, as long as they are able to lower the boom if the job is not being done properly. Former Secretary of HUD, George Romney, in the depths of his disenchantment with the federal bureaucracy, went before a Congressional committee with a three-foot stack of paper representing the red tape involved in processing a *single* grant for a *single* community for a *single* HUD project. This is insane. It is no wonder that after six or seven years and hundreds of millions of dollars of model city legislation we don't have a single model city, or even a model neighborhood, in America.

The granting process and dealing with the federal

government is like playing the game of Monopoly. Every time you go around the board, you never know if you will get your two hundred dollars for passing *Go,* win second prize in a beauty contest, or go immediately to jail. Figuratively speaking, I don't think it matters a damn if a state doesn't observe all the bureaucratic niceties as long as the end results are satisfactory. It's like Adolf Carlson and the twelve-dollar-and-eighty-cent travel check. While Finance and Control is analyzing the minutiae of expense accounts, a whole program may be wasting its total appropriation by not doing what it was intended to do. Monitor the results. Don't monitor the day-to-day expend-itures. Keep a big stick in hand to beat the states that don't want to comply. But don't tie the hands of the states that *do* with so much red tape that they lose heart, initiative, and momentum long before they reach their destinations.

Ours is a system of checks and balances. From our earliest school days, we are taught to think of these as operating entirely at the federal level as between the executive, legislative, and judicial branches. Our national agony of 1973 and 1974 was in part a result of a series of disputes regarding the rights and responsibilities of these three branches as they impinge on one another. But there is a fourth check and balance, and it is the people, not only as they are heard through letters to their congress-men, or in public opinion polls, but the people as they are organized into states. Increasingly, the states are becoming more effective spokesmen for the wishes of their citizens. Their governors are gaining in importance as leaders of a fourth branch of government and becoming mediators between national policy and local administration.

Somewhere between Big Brother and Daddy Warbucks, the federal government has a role in maintaining the dynamic processes of a free society. But not at the cost of draining the dynamism from the states. Ira Sharkansky says, "Ours is a system that rests on the expectations that institutions will pursue their *own* interests and requires other institutions to prod and check their actions." [32] This is a fair description of how our federal system works and how the states should fit within this system.

Most of what happens in our society, happens at the local level, where the people live, where the jobs are, where the land is, where the schools teach, where the smoke comes out of the stack and the sewage flows into the river. Except where constitutional rights are involved, or where local activities affect the health, safety and welfare of others beyond local boundaries, the states must be accorded sufficient respect and given sufficient responsibility to govern and administer themselves. More than that, I believe the burden of proof is on the federal government to demonstrate clear need and no other reasonable solution before it imposes on every state the kind of regulation and control we have become accustomed to accept regularly and docilely along with the dollars that come to sweeten our cup of gall.

For the first time in a generation, revenue sharing is giving the states needed dollars without the imposition of the categorical restrictions, mandated guidelines, or rigid formulas which have characterized most federal-state programs in the past. As important as revenue sharing is in principle, however, it will fail in practice if the Water Quality syndrome prevails.

As Commissioner of Environmental Protection, I believed that Connecticut citizens and its industry wanted a clean state and desired to live up to the law in making and keeping it that way. I may not have been 100 percent right in that approach, but I believe I was at least 90 percent right, and the law gave me the ability to deal promptly and fairly with the other 10 percent.

This is the kind of attitude our national lawmakers and bureaucrats must begin to display. The states, too, want justice, equality, and freedom. They, too, want a better life for all their people. General revenue sharing, practiced as I have described, will help 90 percent make progress toward these goals. And, as in Connecticut, the federal government has enough fiscal and legislative clout to keep the other 10 percent in line to get the national job done.

CHAPTER 7

The Fourth Branch
of Government

★

The first lesson the budding bureaucrat learns at any level of government is the profusion of "life forms" and institutional systems he must deal with. Nothing about government is neat and well-organized. Between the formulation of law, its passage, its funding, and its administration is a host of public agencies, private interests, partisan jealousies, and legal and extralegal checkpoints to be reckoned with. And very often, there are no simple mechanisms for coping. Which is why, I suppose, government has not only been called "an art," but one of extraordinarily modest ambition—"the art of the possible." It is also why very few businessmen, coming to government from an ordered and rational system, can make the adjustment easily.

Consider that in the United States, there are approximately eighty thousand legally established and recognized governmental entities, each with its own officialdom and authority. To a greater or lesser degree, all of these perform services, administer and/or regulate the actions of people, and have the power to raise money. Pity the public official who has to deal with some or all of the nation's three thousand counties, seventeen thousand towns and townships, eighteen thousand municipalities, twenty-one thousand school districts and twenty-one thousand non-school special districts.

In Connecticut, state officials have the burden of selling to one hundred sixty-nine individual town and city governments the idea that proposed statewide policies and programs are good for them. (How fortunate that we are somewhat less complicated than the Chicago metropolitan area which, with a population almost the same as Connecticut's, has an average of one local government for every three square miles, or every five thousand five hundred fifty inhabitants. In all, this area has one thousand, one hundred ninety-eight separate units of government which run schools, regulate transportation, control mosquitoes, or, in some cases, do absolutely nothing at all.)

When I became Commissioner of Environmental Protection, I thought we had won substantial victories when laws were passed. But I quickly found that state legislators can't speak or act for the local officials who, in many districts, really determine how and if the legislation is to be carried out.

Take the state's approach to the solid waste problem, for example. When our statewide solid waste system was being developed, we were quickly brought face to face with the long-standing and inherent distrust the towns had for state programs. No matter how often we sat down with local representatives, we got the same fishy stares and dubious shrugs. They'd been through it all before, they said. The state would impose some program, usually not fund it, and then lay down so many conditions and regulations that were not practical or even applicable, that they were hard-pressed to obey the spirit of the law, much less its letter. They had a waste problem *now,* they told us, with no time for state shenanigans. Who would help pay? And how was the job to get done?

The cities claimed that even with reapportionment, they were suffering from legislative neglect. The smaller towns protested that the state was out to give them a dose of urban problems, and they didn't want any part of it. They all agreed that the state was a big brother they'd just as soon not have in the family.

Long before the solid waste legislation was drafted in final form, we sent a team out into the various regions of the state to explain what we were trying to do and how the towns could benefit from the solid waste program as planned. From these discussions, we learned one very obvious, but easily overlooked, lesson about intergovernmental regulations. The town is the level of government closest to the people. Therefore, it feels rightly that it is most representative of the will of the people and must be most responsive to them. At the state level, the problems that had to be solved were beyond the capability of local government, both financially and organizationally. But imposing solutions on the towns works poorly, if at all.

The Act creating Connecticut's Solid Waste System was explicitly written to be permissive and not mandatory. It offered the towns a service if they wanted to use it, with both functional and economic incentives going into the system. The result? They didn't believe us. These Connecticut Yankees looked at us as if we'd just tried to sell them a wooden nutmeg. They couldn't conceive of the state—way up there in Hartford—proposing a new law that not only had no strings attached but was designed to provide a genuine service and benefits with funding. It was like the suspicion which greets that phrase in insurance advertising, "no agent will call."

After several head-to-head sessions, we convinced town officials we meant what we said. And in the last analysis, when it came to the legislative crunch, virtually every town supported the bill, the state's Conference of Mayors, under the very able leadership of Fairfield's John Sullivan, endorsed it unanimously, the town managers did likewise, and the legislature passed the Solid Waste Act overwhelmingly.

From this experience, I learned that the burden of proof is always on the state to demonstrate to its subdivisions that the issue in question is beyond their capability to solve either economically or functionally. A regional, cooperative approach offers economies of scale, but also leaves local options open just so long as state policy is met.

The burden is on the federal government to demonstrate in the same way to the states that a given problem is national in scope and best handled out of Washington. Where the equities are almost balanced, the decision should always go to that governmental subdivision nearest to the people. This hasn't happened much in the past as each higher level of government has sought to build its own kingdom on the remains of representative, responsive government.

This is why I am opposed in principle to statewide zoning as a solution to land use planning. Until the state can prove that the imposition of statewide policy is necessary to protect the best interests of all the people, I believe land-use decisions should be made—subject, of course, to overall national and state policy—where the land and the interests derived from it are located.

And that is why I believe also that the state should give its subdivisions, especially its cities, more flexibility in creating legislation, and more versatility in taxing power to deal with their highly individualistic local problems. Beyond this, the states should take the lead in fostering Constitutional revision and initiating legislative action to permit cities and towns to reorganize themselves into metropolitan entities more suitable for dealing with the near fatal urban and suburban crises than today's jungle of overlapping governments permits. This will require both a "New Federalism" and a "New Statism." But even before formal mechanisms are established, the states must exhibit both the desire and the willingness to see their urban problems solved—something they have not yet demonstrated very persuasively.

Connecticut's solid waste legislation established an entirely new public-private entity, the Connecticut Resource Recovery Authority, which would direct and oversee the design, building, and operation of the two hundred fifty million dollar system without threatening the political autonomy or financial structure of the towns, and would pay for the system without threatening the fiscal integrity of the state.

Through the statewide solid waste mechanism, the tough political problems of intertown rivalry were eliminated. Before the solid waste legislation was passed, towns in Connecticut had found it difficult to get together to solve any problem that transcended their borders. And because the state has the resources and constitutional capability to finance a technologically advanced solution to their common waste problem, a political liability has been turned into an asset. Under the new Resource Recovery Program, each regional facility will be clean and nonpolluting. Solid waste will be separated into its marketable components of energy and material at the regional separation centers, leaving only inert residue for the new sanitary landfills. And it will all be accomplished at a cost roughly 60 percent of what the aggregate of Connecticut towns would have had to spend over the next fifteen years each going its own way.

If this sort of cooperative resource sharing and public-private partnership works for trash, it can work equally well for more vital, human problems: problems like housing, health, urban jobs, mass transportation, and other problems which many states are now avoiding and local governments are too weak and fragmented to tackle. Revenue sharing with the state and through the state to cooperating "Social" Resource Recovery regions seems to me one very practical solution to the urban crisis. Here is a carrot to persuade communities to work together with adequate funding and the stick of nondelivery of certain services if they turn aside from their responsibility. Poverty and race are issues far less inert and more politically troublesome than trash. But the model is available.

It seems clear to me that imposed and arbitrary regulation is the greatest obstacle to more effective working relationships between the states and their subdivisions. Generally, local government wants to do the right thing. Often it doesn't know what the right thing is, and, more often, it can't afford to do it. The state must take responsibility for both these causes of failure. Through clearcut policy, promptly and effectively communicated, it must establish the rationale on which local decisions can be based. These can be social, environmental, economic or political but they must be clearly propounded and upheld. Once policy is set, the state must make it possible for its subdivisions to uphold the policy. It is hypocritical and damaging to morale for the state to pass laws which it either knows are unworkable or which it refuses to enforce or fund. The state must develop enabling legislation and incentives that will encourage local governments to organize and finance the execution of broad policy as long as it is in the best interests of their citizens. And at the same time the state must have at its disposal a system of penalties and disincentives which will discourage local subdivisions from evading the execution of policy.

To accomplish this, there must be a state legislature that regards itself as truly representative of the "fourth branch of government," the state-local mix that flavors and enriches the marble cake of federalism. Even with reapportionment there is a tendency for state representatives to see themselves as defenders of their various local constituencies rather than upholders of a statewide excellence.

The Environmental Committee of the Connecticut Legislature was a superb example of this broadening process. After a year of close association with the state's severe environmental problems, its members were almost completely accustomed to thinking and innovating in broad concepts rather than narrow parochial channels.

The establishment of a department in the state government totally dedicated to the solution of environmental problems with which the Committee of the legislature could identify was clearly important. There was no place for the legislators to hide. Other state Commissions like Health or Transportation tend to be so broad and so varied in their responsibilities that legislative committee members spend too much of their time dealing with generalities rather than with the specific problems.

One solution to legislative neglect for the urban crisis, for example, might be the formation of a clearly defined and mandated Urban Affairs Department. Like the Environmental Protection Department, its activities would have a single focus—the cities—on which the attention of both bureaucrats and lawmakers would be fixed. Given this kind of exposure, even the most rurally oriented legislator would become involved. Inevitably, he would identify with the cities. And ultimately, I believe, he would find himself, out of simple justice, responding to their needs.

In virtually every state there are certain special problems of a local nature but with statewide implications which are being permitted to fall between the cracks of legislative indifference and executive neglect. One of these is mass transit. Instead of making it the unwelcome stepchild of agencies overwhelmingly concerned with highways and seduced by the 90 percent federal highway funding that forces us into "more" not "balanced" transportation, mass transit deserves a committee of its own outside the jurisdiction of the conventional highway department or transportation bureaucracy.

In Connecticut the governor has appointed a Commission on the Preservation of Agricultural Land. The land is local but the need to preserve the unique urban, suburban, and rural fabric of Connecticut, with agricultural land as the key mortise, is statewide. It is my hope that the next legislature will establish a separate authority (similar to the Resource Recovery Authority), separately funded, to meet this uniquely local yet statewide opportunity to preserve what is Connecticut's fundamental heritage.

One key reason for the establishment of the Resource Recovery Authority was to create an independent mechanism—free not only to develop a system of solid waste disposal but to finance and execute it as well. Although the charge is different and more varied, a Mass Transit Authority, or an Urban Life Authority or an Agricultural Land Authority on the state level could be equally effective.

Some experiments with a similar type of mechanism are being carried out on a local or regional basis with promising results. The Greater Hartford Process, for example—funded almost completely by local business with some federal and state aid—has been organized as a social service agency in tandem with its own development corporation so that physical *and* human renewal of neighborhoods can be carried out simultaneously. But unless these limited demonstrations become part of or in better partnership with the state machinery, their impact and value will be only modest, if at all.

As in the case of waste disposal, local solutions may no longer be completely adequate. It is up to the states, in partnership with their subdivisions, to institutionalize the attack on deep-seated problems. But for practice, let them begin with such relatively noncontroversial areas as solid waste. Then, as they gain experience in true state-local coordination, let them turn their attention and commit their resources to the more complex social issues.

Although state governments focus their attention primarily downward to their own subdivisions and upward to the federal presence, every now and then it is necessary for the state to glance sideways to its relationship with another state or group of states. Interstate cooperation always sounds like a reasonable idea until it is attempted. And then, because of the basic sovereignty accorded each state under the Constitution, the progress of interstate relations, like that of true love, rarely runs smooth.

One reason for this is the fact that no state stands in a position superior to any other under the Constitution. By failing to designate any state by name and by not giving special powers or prerogatives to any one, the Constitution proclaims that all states are equal regardless of size, wealth, population, or resources. They all have the same amount of power reserved to them. Likewise, they all have the same limitations placed upon them. This is one of the glories of our federal system, but it also creates difficulties. Under the Constitution, a republican form of government is guaranteed to every state, and although there is a provision for the formation of new states, none, according to Article Four, "shall be formed within the jurisdiction of any other state nor . . . formed by the junction of two or more states or parts of states without the consent of the legislatures of the states concerned as well as of Congress." The states then are as indestructible and as eternal as the Union itself. The Governor of Rhode Island stands on level ground with the Governor of New York. The Governor of Texas, as flamboyant as he may wish to be, is exactly as influential in terms of the federal system as the

Governor of Kansas, who may be less colorful. When conflicts between the states arise, there is a constitutional mechanism for solving these not by sanctions or force of arms, but by the "judicial power" of the United States.

To preserve the integrity of the federal union, the framers of the Constitution provided that "no two or more states shall enter into any treaty, confederation, or alliance whatever between them without the consent of the United States in Congress assembled." While the intent of this section may have been negative, it has been interpreted over the years as an affirmative grant of power to the states to make such compacts with one another with the consent of Congress.

There are many good reasons why such compacts are useful. Some problems demand bi-state cooperation (or federal intervention) or else the problems will not be solved. For instance, New Jersey and Delaware worked out a compact so that the Delaware Memorial Bridge, at the southern terminal of the New Jersey Turnpike, could be built to replace the overtaxed and archaic ferries that formerly carried motorists from one state to the other. In other cases, it seems to make eminent sense to approach the solution to problems in a regional rather than a fragmented way. With this in mind a number of interstate river basin commissions have been created, such as the New England River Basins Commission, serving as advisor to the coordinating of states' responsibilities for the majestic Connecticut River. Yet in my experience, no region, district or interregional grouping has the weight, power, or clout of a single state which is sovereign within its own borders and constitutionally recognized in its relation to the federal government. Simply stated, unless separately funded and managed, these combinations of states are only part of a solution because in the final analysis they can be no more than single purpose or advisory.

Even though the federal government has been less than successful in attempting to organize social and economic development programs on a regional basis, the states themselves are continuously in contact with one another in the solution of day-to-day problems. On an administrative level, regional consultation is a common practice. Governors, attorneys general, and department heads whose responsibilities transcend state lines not only consult one another but are part of innumerable interstate organizations which pool experience and share knowledge. State legislatures were slow to recognize the advantages of this kind of cross fertilization, but today on both a regional and a national basis legislators are exploring common state problems. There are also organizations, like the Center for State Legislative Research and Service and the Citizens Center on State Legislatures, which perform valuable studies and make recommendations under contract to legislative bodies throughout the nation.

On a less formal basis, Ira Sharkansky speaks of a "follow-the-regional-leader" communications network that prevails among most states which enables the states to reduce their dependence on the federal bureaucracy and encourages the creation of innovative regional solutions.[33]

Both theoretically and practically, these compacts and cross fertilizations are extremely important. As the states turn to each other for ideas and develop practical working relationships, they strengthen themselves as a true fourth branch of government without sacrificing the autonomy or individuality which is the true source of their power.

It is essential, however, that these regional and national interstate relationships develop internally and independently of the federal government. Traditionally, it is Washington which has called the tune on interstate groupings, making them little more than puppets dangling on the strings of government funding with only the barest pretense of power or independence.

The federal experiment with regional Economic Development Commissions is a good case in point. Washington organized them, funded them, established their offices in the nation's capital, appointed a federal co-chairman to run them and gave him an absolute veto which undercut completely the votes of the governors who served on the Commissions. More than three-quarters of the states have been part of the Regional Economic Development Areas. But, as one analyst of the system has pointed out, "the state partners are subject to the *Animal Farm* theory of intergovernmental relations in which all are equal except the federal partner which is a little more equal than the states." As a result, the Economic Development Commissions have been only half as effective as they could have been with firmer state leadership.

Even though "New Federalism," fueled by its revenue sharing programs, has not had an adequate chance to prove itself, it is already placing a higher degree of discretion in the states than any of the old hyphenated organizations which provided only the illusions of independence. Like company unions, they created an impression of power-sharing without any relinquishment of the reins of power. They were federally created, federally financed, federally operated and federally controlled, which has been true of most federal-state relationships over the past forty years. I believe, however, that this kind of demeaning charade is on the way out as the states themselves are asserting their rights to full participation in national policy, and in playing the executive role with sophistication and skill. As state service attracts a higher caliber of civil servant, as state legislatures become better staffed, better paid, and more professionalized, as reapportionment breaks the stranglehold of "downstate" feudalism, as revenue sharing and tax reform give the states a higher degree of solvency, as the governor's office grows in importance—all of which are taking place rapidly throughout the fifty states—I believe we will find in the states a healthy new countervailing force, closer to the people than the House of Representatives, more reflective of their concerns than the Domestic Council, and better able to advise (if lacking the power of consent) than the Senate of the United States.

This is a force that any president is going to have to reckon with and a power that the governors are going to have to take very seriously. The fact that they are beginning to recognize their changing role can be seen in the changing agendas of the Governors' Conference whose secretariat is the Council of State Governments. Organized in 1908 in the administration and with the blessing of Theodore Roosevelt, the Conference and its partisan and regional subdivisions have continued to meet regularly. In the past, the Conference has been concerned primarily with the issues of diminished state power and the encroachments of the national government on states' rights and responsibilities.

While these continue to be relevant topics, meetings are becoming important forums for the expression of public sentiment regarding national policy over a broad spectrum of issues, both national and international, not merely "states' rights."

But this is the "Big Picture." On a day-to-day basis, it does not influence the states in their contacts with one another. At the bureaucratic level, each state must feel its way through a mine field of red tape, parochialism, and insensitivity to the needs of neighbors. Considering the alternatives, these attitudes and practices are probably a fair price to pay for state sovereignty. But to the public official who wants to get a job done, they can often be a nightmare. The founding fathers were wise, indeed, when they placed a Constitutional ban on a state's right to go to war with its neighbors. Former Connecticut Lieutenant Governor T. Clark Hull, a unique public servant and human being, used to jest that when Governor Meskill was away he planned to call out the militia and "march on Massachusetts." On more than one occasion, I wished he would.

An enlightening episode in interstate relations was the "Bacillus Thuringiensis Caper" which brought home to me forcefully both the opportunities and frustrations of the "regional compact."

A few years ago, I decided to experiment on my own farm with an organic pesticide spray called "B.T." (Bacillus Thuringiensis) which is effective against elm spanworms, and partially against gypsy moths, but does not destroy their natural predators or other forms of life.

The brief test run was successful. Beginning with this experiment and followed by other supporting data developed by the Connecticut Agricultural Experiment Station at New Haven, we promulgated statewide regulations banning aerial spraying of all broad spectrum, chemical pesticides (such as DDT) for nonagricultural uses and most agricultural uses. When we began using "B.T." to spray our own state parks and forests, we discovered that the economic justification for chemical spraying was totally fallacious let alone environmentally unsound.

Habit is hard to break. In the second year of our program we discovered that Rhode Island and New York, our good neighbors, were not only permitting broad spectrum chemical spraying but even using these pesticides themselves. Of course, their spraying close to Connecticut's borders was being carried across to our trees, killing our insects and undoing much of the benefit produced by our regulations in those bordering areas.

When we tried to act, however, we discovered that there is very little official machinery available to enjoin the behavior of another sovereign state. There is no United Nations to appeal to. Legal proceedings are long and cumbersome, and the suggestion that we alert Connecticut's Air National Guard to drive off the interlopers was rejected out of hand.

And so we contacted the Environmental Protection Agencies of both states and sent advisors to their hearings on chemical spraying. While we were unsuccessful in changing their practices, we did get agreement that chemical spraying would not take place within one thousand feet of our borders. Today, while our neighbors still persist in what we consider to be an uneconomic and environmentally unsound practice, they are at least respecting Connecticut's territorial integrity. Since there is historical evidence of states following the examples of their more enlightened neighbors, we have every reason to hope that Rhode Island and New York will inevitably ban the use of broad spectrum pesticides, too.

As a footnote to the incident, the federal government was so distressed by our failure to use chemical sprays that it threatened to quarantine our parks and forests and forbid vacationers to use them. But fortunately in this case, we were able to "convince" the U.S. Department of Agriculture that our protective measures were adequate, and that leaving some insects alive was not a threat but a benefaction. (I shouldn't say "convince." We simply told them where to go, which, since we never heard from them again, I assume they did.)

When incidents occur like the "Bacillus Thuringiensis Caper" or the attempts of other New England states to change the course, amount or quality of the water in the Connecticut River which flows from Vermont to Long Island Sound, there is some justification for wondering if state sovereignty is not obsolete. Governor Sanford tells of a noted newspaper columnist who asked him why it wouldn't be preferable for all the New England states to merge into one. Governor Sanford's answer is instructive. "It won't work for a lot of reasons," he said, "but the simplest is that they are not going to give up ten of their twelve Senators" [34]—or five of their six governors, for that matter.

No one state has a monopoly on character, wisdom, or virtue. But every state has its own vigorous mix of strengths and weaknesses which are very much worth preserving. Each has its own unique combination of people, places and traditions, too, and these provide the bone and sinew that give America its shape and form. I always found it interesting and instructive to share experiences with my counterparts in other state governments. But, somehow, I felt a sense of comfort and relief when I returned to dealing with Connecticut people and Connecticut problems.

Call it provincialism or chauvinism. Whatever its name, it runs deep in Americans of every state. In Ethan Allen's often quoted words inscribed on the wall of the Capitol of Vermont it is both explained and justified: "I am as determined to preserve the independence of Vermont as Congress is that of the Union, and rather than fail I will retire with my hearty Green Mountain Boys into the caverns of the mountains and wage war on all mankind."

In today's cool world, Ethan Allen's rhetoric may sound overblown, but this fierce pride in home is important to understand and cherish. It is the unique genius of each state that helps keep alive the independence and individual autonomy which preserve us as a free people. It is through the union of these prideful states as a fourth branch of government that a balance is maintained between broad national interests and our strongly held, though often threatened, personal rights. It is both a sovereignty worth defending and a union worth preserving.

CHAPTER 8

Mind Your Own
State's Business

★

A few years ago, Tom McCall, the former Governor of Oregon greeted a national convention in Portland. "We welcome you to our state," he said, "and want you to enjoy yourselves while you are here. But when your convention is over, we hope you will go back home and forget about living here permanently."

A year later, this same governor was discouraging even visitors to his state. Too many people, too many automobiles, too much careless use of parks and forests were spoiling the way of life the people of Oregon had chosen for themselves. The governor felt he was responding to a mandate to keep Oregon for Oregonians.

In Vermont, land-use legislation has made an important start toward reducing the vacation-home land rush and ski-resort sweepstakes which were rapidly converting this lovely, rural New England state into a prefabricated exurb for city-weary residents of New York and the industrialized Northeast.

Hawaii and Florida have enacted laws similar to Vermont's. California has voted to restrict severely all further development along the state's one thousand one hundred-mile coastline. Oregon, too, has beginning land-use laws and coastline restrictions. Other states with precious and fragile resources of natural beauty, uncluttered calm, or recreational pleasure are also taking action. Colorado, in an unprecedented referendum in 1972, rejected a bid to hold the 1976 Winter Olympics in its state. Advocates of the "No" vote argued that the Olympics would produce irreversible environmental damage, crowding, and the destruction of natural surroundings in return for a few extra dollars in the pockets of profit-hungry entrepreneurs. Out of respect for the long-term preservation of Colorado's natural heritage, the people of the state refused to be seduced by visions of a questionable economic bonanza.

In Connecticut, a three-year battle by aroused environmentalists halted the planned construction of a segment of Interstate 291. This connector would have facilitated commuter traffic within the Hartford area while maintaining and reinforcing old patterns of land use. And it would have impinged upon a reservoir and forest area highly prized by the residents of the region. Instead, the capital region will be the subject of a probing, interdisciplinary land-use–transportation study, more broadly encompassing than the narrow, simplistic option of road-no road.

The proliferation of incidents like these suggests that state and local sovereignty is not extinct; that the legislatures and the people are far from the moribund condition Frank Trippett described when he accused them of "exhibiting precious little vitality and precious little concern." [35] The states are very much alive and fighting for their identity and their integrity.

The fact is that Americans are beginning to resist all melting pot theories and practices. Ethnicity and national culture are being strongly defended against bureaucratic attacks by departments of education, welfare and housing. Some Blacks, Indians, Puerto Ricans, and Mexican-Americans are demanding their right to preserve the integrity of their customs even though total assimilation might appear to offer the most direct opportunities for economic and social progress.

In a sense, this emphasis on pluralism is one reason why the concept and programs of the Great Society have failed. Bland, blanket slogans do not describe the variety of people and experiences our country contains. Good neighborhoods are more important than a Great Society, and these can only be produced by the people of the neighborhoods themselves, not by remote social planners seeking to impose some unrealizable platonic ideal of a neighborhood.

Similarly, citizens of states with precious forest and wilderness areas, open space, farms, and historic sites—patterns of traditional land use which are the fabric of a state—are fighting to keep their way of life from becoming engulfed by the national trend toward wall-to-wall developments, highways, and people.

In part, the relentless conversion of America to a uniform ticky-tacky spread of shopping centers, gas stations, motels, and ready-to-eat restaurants has been slowed down. The energy crisis, the visible disasters of environmental degradation, runaway urbanization, and the sheer overcrowding of all recreational facilities and natural areas have combined to produce a state-led movement for a simpler, cleaner life, which attempts to balance economic, social and environmental concerns. And this, in turn, has created public demand for accountability and action by those state and local officials who were elected to office and who, by God, can be voted out of office if they betray the vision of a quality of life they were elected to protect.

How to weigh and balance the needs of the people against the resources available to sustain them is a question topping the agenda of government at every level. And within the framework of the Constitution and the limitations imposed by federal law, it is one of the major pieces of business that the states must consider and act upon.

We have invented a phrase, "quality of life," to describe this precarious equation. Overuse has already made it a cliché. But "quality of life" is exactly what the people are looking to their states to protect and preserve. A recent Louis Harris poll indicates that most Americans look to Washington for the survival aspects of their personal lives. Larger issues on which the life of the country itself depends—national defense, the national economy, foreign trade, the monetary system—these the public expects the federal government to resolve.

But in those crucial sectors of responsibility that determine how well, how comfortably, how securely we are going to live—housing, education, transportation, law and order, environment, welfare, health—the state and local divisions of government are perceived as the prime sources of both policy and its execution.

So, minding the states' business is not by any means the dying occupation that some critics of our federal system would have us believe. In fact, as an already deep-seated disenchantment with the federal government grows and darkens, the people are going to expect more and demand more of those state and local officials who are most immediately accountable to them.

This will be especially true in every area of decision-making where quality of life is concerned. Direct accountability rather than bureaucratic posturing will have to be observed by any local official who expects to keep both his job and the public trust. This will not be easy. Executive privilege and party loyalty are not frivolous customs. They make possible civility and cooperation between the various branches of government. But in situations where candor and responsiveness are required to maintain the confidence of the people, a more direct and open approach will be demanded. If there is any single Watergate lesson, this is it.

My own trial by fire came during the heightened

controversy over the construction of I-291 referred to previously. Because the governor had come out strongly in favor of the road, I felt I was in no position to undercut his authority or to damage his credibility. To the environmental activists for whom the road had become the most compelling issue of the day, my position seemed ambiguous at best. The department had conducted a preliminary study of the environmental impact of the highway. From this, we had concluded that there were serious objections to its construction, not so much because it might damage the ecosystem 100 yards to the left and right of the road, but because of more complex effects on the community, its population growth and density, the dislocation of people and the impact on their health and ultimate safety.

I transmitted our reservations to the governor, and to the state and federal Departments of Transportation. But I did not feel, in the light of contrary views expressed by members of the state government, that I should take a public position diametrically opposed to theirs short of resigning to do so.

So I worked behind the scenes to persuade the governor and the Department of Transportation that not only I-291, but all highway construction in the region should be subjected to a comprehensive land-use–transportation study. This would take into consideration all aspects of construction and usage and weigh the probable trade-offs involved in a multiplicity of complex highway decisions vs. present and projected land use.

Like so many before me, I found this a tough position. I felt that if I had projected myself as a simple, saintly advocate of the environmental position only, I might have pleased one element of my constituency, but I would have made the governor and his Commissioner of Transportation look like either villains or fools or both. If that had happened, my department would have lost permanently its ability to be effective on the broad front of environmental

policy and action. It would have been cast in an adversary
role. The governor would have been forced to react. In
sheer self-defense, the Department of Transportation
would have withdrawn its cooperation, and, while we
might have won the battle of I-291, we would have
damaged our ability to fight even more important battles
that lay ahead.

What happened? The newspapers got hold of my letter
to the state Department of Transportation on the highway's environmental impact. In addition, I was violently
attacked by the antihighway advocates for not leading a
"Ban the Road Bike Ride" around the reservoir to
dramatize the issue. "Lufkin Weak on Highway" was the
headline in a local newspaper. But at the end of the
political and procedural road, everything happened as I
had hoped. The governor halted construction of I-291. The
environmentalists transferred their attentions to another
piece of highway construction. And our long-sought and
comprehensive land-use–transportation study of trade-offs
got under way.

As I look back now, I may have erred on the side of
bureaucratic cooperation. I really don't know the answer.
Perhaps all public servants should be totally candid in
letting the people know precisely where they stand. The
trouble is, quality of life issues, or any issues for that
matter, are rarely simple ones. Analysis of trade-offs can
be subtle and imprecise. Frequently, one's own administrative point of view is too limited to bear the weight of a
major political decision. And public confrontation is the
single worst platform to solve any problem, that I know.

Rarely is the perspective of quality of life the same for
every segment of society. Roads must inevitably be built
or we will return to a provincial economy capable of
sustaining only a relatively small population. Mass transit
is a highly desirable alternative, but it is years ahead of us
and, at best, will be able to solve only a fraction of our

nation's logistical requirements due to historic patterns of land use already in place.

Quality of life is imprecise and in some instances indefinable. The official who believes that he can satisfy everyone's definition is in for some shocking disappointments. Oregon, for example, had little difficulty in passing a landmark "Beverage Container Act" which not only banned the use of nonreturnable disposable bottles in the state but outlawed metal containers "so designed and constructed that a part of the container is detachable in opening the container without the aid of a can opener."

Needless to say, environmentalists in Connecticut—another environmentally sophisticated state—were quick to propose a similar Bottle Bill calling for mandatory deposits on bottles and, ultimately, a ban on all but returnable beverage containers. Here, too, I was caught on the horns of the quality of life dilemma. Every instinct cried out that the bill was good, necessary and inevitable. There is simply no justification for the waste of resources and the pollution of land and water resulting from throwaway bottles and the discarded lids of flip-top cans.

But there was another side of the issue to be considered. Unlike Oregon, where 50 percent of the bottles were still of the returnable variety when the legislation was passed, Connecticut's were virtually 100 percent nonreturnable. What steps should be taken to resolve the serious economic dislocation and potential unemployment resulting from such a bill in Connecticut? What about the imposition of an additional charge per bottle which would drive many people across conveniently close state lines to buy their beverages elsewhere? What of the Connecticut retailers selling such merchandise? And what of the small bottlers, of which the state has many, who would be forced to shut down because—unlike their big competitors—they could not immediately install and activate recyclable bottle lines? And what of the bottle manufacturers pro-

ducing nonreturnable bottles within the state? Was there
no consideration to be given to their welfare?

I am not saying that there was a total balancing of
equities in this case. There never is. If I had been an
environmental lobbyist, not a state official, I would have
been at the barricades fighting for a strong Bottle Bill. But,
as part of state government, I had to give consideration to
all the diverse elements comprising Connecticut's quality
of life: economic, social, financial as well as environmental.

I tried to communicate my own position to the environmental constituency. I supported such legislation. But at
the same time, I was advocating a year-and-a-half delay in
the effective date of the legislation so that we could work
out all the technical, economic, and environmental problems. This would put the bottlers on notice, shifting to
them the onus of figuring out an equitable solution to a
piece of pending but not immediate legislation.

There are times of crisis when changes in practice must
be made immediately regardless of their secondary impact.
Partisans of any given issue are always demanding "now."
But administering the state's business is a more subtle
balancing act requiring time to adjust to the conflict
between "now" and "later" which can only be resolved by
mutual tolerance and understanding.

Peter Drucker says that, by and large, businessmen
spend 90 percent of their time concentrating on problems
and 10 percent of their time concentrating on opportunities. The same ratio applies to government. The responsibility of government at every level is to enlarge the
opportunities of those being governed. This is especially
true at the state and local level where the impact of
government decision-making is most directly and immediately felt. It is to the opportunity areas—those that define
and determine quality of life—that state resources should
be most generously assigned. And while it is simplistic to

say that problems are only opportunities in disguise, I have found that this small but vital shift in perspective is often enough to foster an atmosphere in which can be developed creative solutions to situations that once seemed unmanageable.

One of the most persuasive arguments for revenue sharing is its potential for funding new approaches by state government to deeply entrenched human problems which have not been solved by blanket federal programs. And not only not solved, but in many instances made worse by the grandiose "solve all problems at once" approach. Under previous categorical grant systems, each state has had to adjust its unique perspective to meet specific if broad national guidelines. Connecticut, for the most part, has received the same treatment as New Mexico. Revenue sharing will test the capacity of the states to maintain individual life-styles and approaches while conforming to overall federal policy. For we should not confuse individuality with license or state responsibility with an absolute view of "states' rights." What revenue sharing may force is a greater degree of accountability by state and local governments at all levels to the people in their constituencies rather than to the faceless scorekeepers of some remote Washington bureaucracy. Governor Meskill aptly described these categorical granting establishments as "paragovernmental empires," which exist only because they have access to federal money and limit the states' creativity by attaching the money to tight out-of-state bureaucratic strings.

Revenue sharing, however, will not succeed if the states use it solely to swell their general funds or to reduce taxes. If that's the case, traditional services will be continued at the maintenance level instead of moving up from inadequacy to excellence.

There is no end to the argument that state and local governments are too insensitive to difficult social problems, too vulnerable to advocate politically unpopular solutions. But there is no need to resolve this argument before we give the states the resources to improve their capacity to be responsive and to reduce their dependence on special interests and power groups. There are sufficient mechanisms for obtaining federal intervention when the state's will falters or its humanitarianism bows to expediency. But if the states are not given the chance to protect the uniqueness of their quality of life, the federal government is going to impose upon them its own bland and featureless version. In every instance tried to date, this has been disastrous.

In minding the states' business, the national government has a very legitimate role to play. It must establish the basic rules of the game and enforce minimum standards of fair play which prevent one state from either robbing another of its industry or palming off its poor to another because it doesn't choose to obey the rules. Government already assumes this posture over a broad spectrum of federal legislation for industry, such as minimum wage requirements and safety and health standards. But within these limits which affect everyone, individual businesses are free to set their own rules and to provide workers with even stronger safeguards against sickness or injury if they so choose. In the areas of welfare, education, transportation, and housing for which, according to the Harris poll, the public assigns responsibility to the states, the federal government should establish uniform minimum standards permitting the states individual variations only when these have been met.

Welfare

In the area of welfare, for example, I believe it is the business of the federal government to lay down regulations and set standards which will affect every state equally. It is unconscionable for any state to be able to starve its indigent population into emigration to another state offering higher welfare payments. Yet every day the buses are filled with families with publicly paid one-way tickets arriving at already overcrowded cities from rural states where welfare payments are below subsistence.

While the states should administer a wide variety of programs to improve the condition of their welfare population, the federal government should be responsible for the maintenance of a uniform quality of life that is on a par for welfare recipients throughout the country. The SSI (Supplementary Security Income) guaranteed to the aged, disabled, and blind is a step in the right direction. Beyond the minimum standard guaranteed by the federal government, the citizens of each state should be free to decide how much more, and in what ways, they wish to augment the national norms. Under SSI, states can add to the benefits given by the federal government, but they cannot reduce the minimum guaranteed. Although it does not include aid to dependent children, SSI is a beginning toward alleviating the present injustice which encourages low economic states to offer the lowest welfare payments because the federal share diminishes as the state contribution grows larger.

I support a federally operated welfare system which assures equity across the nation to recipients as well as to those who must pay for it. Because of the mobility of citizens and the cyclical nature of opportunity in the various states, it is only logical that welfare or income maintenance benefits have the same kind of portability that social security and other federal health and welfare benefits possess and that some private pension plans now possess as well.

Welfare is one area which the public thinks should be controlled and supervised by the states. But with 60 percent of all welfare payments now coming from the federal government, it is clear that the states will never be able to support this program on their own. Furthermore, it has become such an administrative nightmare that few public servants will voluntarily saddle their careers to the bucking bronco of the states' welfare bureaucracy. My colleague, Henry White, an able Connecticut businessman who bravely "submitted" to appointment as Welfare Commissioner, resigned after a turbulent two years in office with the philosophical observation, "Dealing with the federal welfare bureaucracy is like trying to put socks on an octopus." There has to be a better way, and it's up to the federal government in this instance, to provide both policy and funding to lull the octopus into some semblance of submission. To date this has not occurred.

Probably the most effective tranquilizer would be some acceptable version of the Nixon administration's Family Assistance Plan or the Johnson administration's Negative Income Tax, which would replace the nation's one thousand one hundred disparate, overlapping and thoroughly inadequate welfare programs. Within this broad framework, the state's role should be to concentrate on upgrading opportunity and getting people off welfare, rather than on the administration of the present state-federal nightmare.

Education

More than any other area of decision-making, the American people believe that educational policy should be set at the state level and administered by the communities. As with welfare, however, gross inequities in educational opportunity not only exist from state to state but between communities in the same state and districts within the same community. One of the reasons for these inequities lies in our almost total dependence on the local property tax which not only produces serious revenue shortfalls in many communities but varies wildly with the level of effort, the presence of industry, and the percentage of assessed valuation. It is unconscionable that the low income Edgewood School District in San Antonio can raise only thirty-seven dollars per student through property taxes, while the more affluent Alamo Heights District raises four hundred twelve dollars per student, although its residents are taxed at a *lower* rate than Edgewood's.

For a while, in the past two years, it seemed as if suits brought in various states and upheld in state supreme courts would overthrow reliance on the property tax by declaring its educational use unconstitutional. The Serrano decision in California, *Rodriguez vs. San Antonio* in Texas, *Van Dursatz vs. Hatfield* in Minnesota and others seemed to express the principle that, within reason, wealth discrimination due to variances in property tax levels violates the Fourteenth Amendment of the Constitution.

A decision of the Supreme Court overturning the Rodriguez Doctrine has mooted school finance suits brought under this principle in twenty-seven states. The majority of the Supreme Court rejected the theory that free public education is guaranteed under the Fourteenth Amendment. "Education, of course, is not among the rights afforded explicit protection under our federal Constitution," wrote Justice Powell, "nor do we find any basis for saying it is implicitly so protected."

Although the courts in twenty-five states are considering arguments that state constitutions require equalized spending among school districts, the fundamental constitutional challenge has been blunted. Now it is up to the people of the states, through enlightened executive and legislative leadership, to put an end on their own to the economic justification for unequal education.

Perhaps it is too idealistic to depend on individual

conscience to put an end to injustice. But certainly a way must be found to develop a federal policy which will guarantee the eradication of such inequities, which are often based almost entirely on race. In the meantime, I believe that the state should assume at least half of the burden of financing public education within its borders through a method of property tax equalization and redistribution which will assure an acceptable minimum educational standard for all communities, permitting the wealthier districts to tax themselves further to support any local options they may wish to add beyond this point.

A number of states are moving in this direction. In 1971, for instance, Maryland assumed responsibility for full state funding of school construction costs, while Minnesota greatly increased its share of local school costs as part of a comprehensive tax reform package. In 1972, California provided an additional billion dollars in new school funding and property tax relief. And in 1973, Florida, among others, moved to equalize educational funding across the state.

The greatest cause of injustice within some states is the network of racial attitudes which have hardened into local policy. State neglect of the cities is as much a product of racial prejudice as is San Antonio's inability to come to grips with the bankrupt school system in its own Edgewood District, which is overwhelmingly Mexican-American. It is a fatal delusion to believe that such a cancer can be contained forever without weakening and, ultimately, destroying the entire body politic. During the court battle over Edgewood, a resident of the neighborhood was interviewed by the press. "Do you know," she said, "Edgewood's high school has never graduated a student who went on to become a professional man. But we have supplied more than our share of the dead soldiers on San Antonio's scroll of honor."

Many states are actively pursuing a course of improve-

ment in equality of opportunity. On the whole, the states
have a far better record than private industry in minority
employment. And it is my belief that the states and
localities combined do better than the federal government
in this regard. But even well-intentioned employment
policies will flounder if the states do not produce enough
trained and educated citizens to be able to hold down the
increasingly complex jobs our society has to offer.

This is the prime function of each state's school system,
most of which are presently tyrannized by the local
property tax and weakened by largely subconscious racism
which denies money for educational improvement in those
very areas where the need is greatest.

Transportation

When former Governor Cahill of New Jersey had spent
a year in office, he was asked to comment on his most
difficult problem. It was not race, he said, not the cities,
not economic development but transportation. And for
many states, transportation remains an unresolved mess.
There is a general misconception that the federal government funds most highway construction. While it is true
that next to welfare, the states depend on Washington
most to support highway programs, the fact is that only
about one-third of state highway funds come from the
federal government, while the states are spending approximately fifteen billion dollars a year on highway planning
and construction.

The people look to the states to solve their transportation problems, most of which revolve around getting from
here to there in the quickest, most direct way possible,
preferably alone in private automobiles. Although the
energy crisis and the increased price of gasoline may alter
this picture, alternative means of transportation have not
yet received great popular support. Environmentalists may
protest against the placement of highways in ecologically

sensitive areas, but very few of them will pick up the placards and march for mass transit. They may ride bikes to protest an I-291, but chances are they will get to the scene of the protest in an automobile. And for this there really isn't much of an alternative based on past patterns of land use.

This relative disinterest on the part of citizens is mirrored in state expenditures for mass transit. These have been in the neighborhood of one hundred fifty million dollars annually, which is one-hundredth of what the states are spending on highway construction.

The truth of the matter is that very little coherent planning has gone into the whole subject of transportation. Most planning is being done by state highway departments whose activities depend mainly on their reports to the Federal Highway Administration indicating estimates of funds required to construct new highways and to bring existing roads and streets to certain standards. Planning for mass transportation is not encouraged and is virtually nonexistent. Where it does exist, it is totally unrelated to any national plan because no such plan has yet been developed. And it only tangentially focuses on the basis for all transportation–land use.

Rail transportation has been moderately revived by the federal Amtrak agency. In a state like Connecticut, however, there is only modest rail access within the state or between Connecticut and its neighbors. And today the federal government has proposed abandoning one-fourth of all nonpassenger rail lines in Connecticut—rail lines that could be refurbished and tied into both passenger and freight movement for the future.

If mass transit comes about, it will not be at the instigation of state transportation departments which are essentially only renamed highway departments. It will be impelled by external circumstances, such the energy crisis, which is cutting down on fuel consumption, and by

land-use–quality-of-life considerations—the kinds of pressures which killed I-291—in a search for a longer range,
more balanced solution.

Such casual treatment of a highly significant state
problem must not be permitted to continue. The states
must consciously elect to pursue a broad range of alternatives to passenger car transportation and highway construction. Rural domination of state legislatures, which
once decreed disproportionate construction in "down-
state" areas, has been effectively broken. Urban concerns
with mass transit now receive full legislative expression. In
every state, the cities are going to continue exerting
pressure until mass transit becomes a legislative and
executive priority.

As a beginning, the sanctity of the highway trust fund
must be breached to a substantial degree, and this has
begun. Under the gun of shrinking energy supplies and
crowded highways, the automobile companies should
divert an increasing share of their resources to the
development of mass transit systems which, in the long
run, could well provide a substantial market. The "marketing myopia" which caused our oil companies to think of
themselves as being in the oil rather than the energy
business until a few years ago should be fair warning to
our automobile companies to define their transportation
market far more broadly than just cars.

With some measure of enlightened policy coming out of
Congress, the states will be in a better position to tackle
mass transportation on both an inter- and intrastate basis.
I don't expect six hundred miles of Connecticut's obsolete
rail system to be rejuvenated completely. But clearly the
network is there, and rather than abandon such a scheme,
we must find and encourage ways to reclaim it and return
it to service. Transportation is so central to almost every
aspect of "quality of life," I expect that my state, as well as
all others, will give creative consideration to the problems.

Clearly we must come up with worthwhile solutions before we choke on our own fumes, or are forced into shrinking urban enclaves by the very highways we built originally to set us free.

Housing and Land Use

While transportation is a means of getting us from here to there, more people in the states are concerned with the quality of both "here" and "there" than with the method of traveling between them, although the two are clearly intertwined. For most Americans, "here" is home; "there" is work, shopping or recreation, and the straightest, most acceptable line between the two points is a four-lane highway. All points and all lines drawn between them exist on the same plane. All occupy land. And, as population and economic development increase, new points of "here" and "there" must be plotted on state maps and more access routes provided to link them. Unfortunately, these are not simply geometric exercises in a planner's copybook. Every new home, business site, shopping center, school and recreation area, and every road between must be gouged out of the living landscape.

The residents of our states know all too well that this landscape is finite. Each day they can measure its subtraction from the whole in felled trees, cleared orchards and meadows, bulldozed forests and farmlands and the inevitable swarm of tractors, spreaders, and cement mixers that cover the wounded landscape like flies on a corpse. And this grim picture becomes ever more poignant when one considers, based on population projections and present age, that we will have to build as much from now to the year 2000 as has been built in this country since the Revolution.

Surveys show that most people look to the state for solutions to the complex problems of "here" and "there" which are categorized generally as "housing." Yet it is in the housing area that they are provided the least satisfactory answers. For the questions of where people are going to live and in what life-style cannot be answered in simple geographical, architectural or even economic terms. No issue is more wrapped in controversy than housing with its social, racial, class, political, and environmental overtones.

Traditionally, the problems of housing have been finessed by the states upward to the federal government and downward to local towns and cities. Washington created and financed public housing for the poor, encouraged home buying among the middle class and made vast loan programs available to stimulate the development of apartments and condominiums when readily accessible land for quarter-acre single-family residences began to dry up.

Through the massive dislocations of population and mushrooming construction of "heres," "theres" and connecting highways which have characterized the generation since World War II, the states have played a relatively passive role. For much of that period, they sat back and enjoyed the benefits of development; the influx of industry and the increase in both taxable income and taxable property. Now, however, the states have been made grimly aware that development has created far more problems than it has solved. The urban crisis is a direct result of suburban development, population shifts, industrial expansion, and the tangled web of zoning regulations which have set neighbor against neighbor, town against town.

Coping with complex housing-related problems often leads to internal dissension and conflicting policy, and the states have been painfully slow to act. But now they are beginning to face up to the realities of more people, less land, environmental pollution, urban decay, and social chaos.

They have started to move forward, at about the same time that funds were frozen for federally assisted housing programs. The typical state-level response has been to create a Housing Development Agency; there are now thirty-six of them, and more are expected. These agencies, generally working indirectly, can float bond issues at relatively low rates, and then turn around and re-loan money at attractive rates for low and moderate income housing. In six states the Housing Development Agencies can acquire land directly, and in three of them, New York, Hawaii, and Delaware, the agencies can carry out direct construction or rehabilitation activities.

New York State's Urban Development Corporation (UDC), led by the formidable Edward J. Logue, has been the most unusual and controversial of these agencies. It has built tens of thousands of units of housing, in ghettos and in cornfields, and has constructed whole new communities from scratch. While the concept is sound, the execution must be well managed like any other business enterprise.

The source of the problem has been that until recent times, we were victimized by the delusion that land is plentiful. Operating under a market theory proclaiming that what is most expensive must be best, we encouraged unrestrained competition for the development of our most desirable land, much of it our best farm land. Giving strict adherence to the first commandment of real estate: "Get the best deal," or "develop to the highest economic use," we sold off our most priceless natural resources to fast-talking, well-heeled developers who promised much, built their new and ill-planned communities and shopping centers, and then departed, leaving the towns, cities, and states holding the bag of increased costs and inadequate facilities.

In our rush to minimize social and economic damage and to slow down random development, a patchwork of public controls and regulations for land use has been put on the books by local councils and state legislatures. Yet these regulations and controls are only stopgap measures to buy us a little time at best. What is really needed is more effective land use planning carried out on behalf of the land and all the people, rather than for the developers and the special interests.

This will require a far greater involvement on the part of the states and local communities than ever before. And, because the pendulum of reaction always swings too far, there will be great pressures for rigid statewide zoning regulations to compensate for ill-conceived local zoning activities.

I am opposed to statewide zoning on the grounds that basic decisions affecting "here" should not be made "there." How a piece of land can be used should not be decreed by those who will not have to suffer the consequences of these land-use decisions. This is one of the main problems we face with almost all of our federal programs. Let's not duplicate it in an area so central to our well-being—to our quality of life. The people of the community in which the land is located should retain the right to determine its use. But, like all other rights, it should be exercised within a framework of responsibility based on the availability of knowledge about the implications of land decisions and stimulated by incentives and penalties established by those governmental agencies which have the larger environmental responsibility.

Connecticut has promulgated a Plan of Conservation and Development which sets forth some guiding principles according to which land-use decisions should be made; in this case using water resources as a standard for planning. However, it was launched without much enthusiasm or support and has not been successful in stimulating discussion much less provoking policy. As with many sensitive areas of regulation, some states will probably have to be prodded into action by the federal government. Land-use legislation was introduced by Senator Jackson and, in the beginning at least, supported by the Nixon administration until effectively killed by the Congress in 1974. It called upon the states to develop plans for "critical areas" and land uses within their boundaries such as "regions" of environmental concern, large-scale developments, key facilities such as airports and developments of regional benefit.

To inspire the states to adopt land-use planning for these areas, the original legislation incorporated a system of incentives and sanctions making it difficult for the states to evade compliance. Power would have been vested in the executive branch to stem the flow of money from three major federal grant-in-aid programs to states that were not cooperating—the Airport and Airways Development Act, various federal highway programs, and the Land and Water Conservation Fund. At this writing, most of the teeth have been extracted from this federal land-use legislation, and the actions of the House of Representatives suggest that no such legislation will be forthcoming in the near future. Even so, it is still essential that federal guidelines be enacted to provide a policy framework within which the states and their subdivisions can plan rationally for further growth.

Land use is an area in which some states themselves are already exercising leadership even in the absence of federal statutes. More than a decade ago, Hawaii enacted a comprehensive zoning plan dividing the state into four classifications: agriculture, conservation, rural, and urban, and established state policy for each of these sectors, to be administered by the local municipalities. Colorado, Vermont, Maine, Florida, and Oregon have passed land-use laws that are a good beginning and many of the other states have adopted controls over certain critical areas of more than local significance, such as coastal zones, shorelines, wetlands and flood plains.

Once such legislation is on the books, the era of

indiscriminate land use will begin to draw to a close, and the threat of universal ghettoization will be lifted. Local communities will have to concentrate on the improvement of quality of life in those regions designated as urban and residential. They will no longer be able to avoid coping with the problems of the cities in the false hope of being able to escape into the suburbs or of creating new suburbs in lands now excluded from development. Planned unit development and cluster housing will be given new incentives. Inevitably, the realities of finite expansion will make exclusionary zoning and racial and class restrictions increasingly impractical to maintain. For if federal and state policy make flight impossible, we will have to stand and face realistically our land-use and housing problems. And this environmental concern, in the broadest sense, rather than social engineering, may very well be the lever we have needed to create decent living environments for all our people, rather than only those who can afford a one-way ticket from the dying cities to the rapidly vanishing countryside.

Welfare, education, transportation, and housing are the four basic "quality of life" issues which the public expects the states to cope with. The federal government is too remote to deal realistically with these issues on a day-to-day basis. And the people are wiser than many of their most advanced theorists in recognizing this fundamental truth. Paul J. Halperin says that "The major substantive issues of the 1970s are fairly clear to us: the relationship of man to his environment, the inequities of America's social and economic life, and the increasing polarization and alienation of the population." [36]

These are the issues which cut closest to the bone. They stalk the streets of our cities and confront us at every turn in our daily lives. They will provide the agenda for the

CHAPTER 9

What the People Think

★

In *United They Fell*, a slashing if not very well documented attack on the ineffectiveness of state government, Frank Trippett says, "It would be preposterous for any working American who has at length attained any voice at shaping his small fraction of the economy to identify at all with the state government. Its history of hostility to the change that social improvement entails has been too persistent and too often dramatized in a way that can be understood even by the unlettered." [38]

The record refutes this superficial verdict. For most of our history the states, not the federal government, have been the primary agents both for social improvement and for the preservation of local customs and mores which the people have wished to retain.

Until Franklin Roosevelt, when the balance of power began shifting dramatically to Washington, individual states operated as major change agents, with the federal government either following along tardily or, through the Supreme Court, declaring such state action unconstitutional. Without experimentation on the part of the states, most of the legislation protecting the economic rights of Trippett's "unlettered" would have been long delayed. If not for enlightened administration by the states, his children would not have enjoyed free public education from kindergarten through university. His mental and physical health would not have been protected as well as they are through state and local hospitals and medical schools. His rights under an equitable system of criminal and civil justice might have been weakened.

The imperfections of state and local government lie not so much with venal legislators or corrupt executives as with the fact that institutional change comes slowly at best. The closer institutions are to the people, the more they reflect their basic conservatism and reluctance to change—in other words, the more they directly reflect the will of the majority they represent.

Local custom, regional prejudice, fear of social and economic displacement are not to be reckoned with lightly. They are social and psychological facts that government must always take into account when charting change. Change is resisted when it comes so fast that old, familiar landmarks are obliterated. The rush of social legislation in the 1960s, pouring pell-mell from the national cornucopia, may have been motivated by the most idealistic intentions. But, inevitably, even the people who lived in the troubled areas that Washington was trying to help all at once demanded a chance to pause for breath. Because of this, they elected a President who promised to place in their hands more power to control the pace and direction of change and to diminish the capacity of the federal government to attempt change by fiat.

Even before I entered state service, I was aware that nothing can arouse the passions of state or local residents so fiercely as the threat of direct change. Whether in tax rates, assessments, school boundaries, zoning regulations, or town budgets, the people come out in force when change is on the agenda. More intellectually or socially significant subjects which are abstract and remote, are never able to draw the same crowds or elicit the same emotion. This discovery reinforced my belief that the people are vitally interested in the decision-making process close at hand, and that not even the emphasis of the media on national and international events can diminish the public's desire to know and participate in what is happening at the local level with those bread and butter issues that directly affect them.

When it comes to international monetary policy and defense spending, the citizen generally counts on his congressional representatives to act in his behalf. Not being a party to committee hearings or White House breakfasts or privy on a daily basis to the *Congressional Record*, the average American is unaware of the extent to which most national legislation will affect him. Until it does.

On the state and local level, however, woe betide the legislator or bureaucrat who sells out a constituent even for what he thinks to be a greater good. Even the most homespun native politician tends to lose the common touch when he is sent to Washington. But the local office holder can't hide his voting record, his occupation or his hometown ties behind the remote façade of a federal office building.

When the Department of Environmental Protection was helping put together a pesticide bill, I was very sensitive to the bill's language as it applied to farmers. As a farmer myself, I know we are among the most careful and attentive users of pesticides. Because of this, I could not see the justification for requiring them to be licensed before they could spray. Caught up in bureaucratic red tape and procedural requirements, they could lose irreplaceable spraying time which could adversely, if not ruinously, affect their crops.

When the bill was released for hearings, it included a federal provision for the licensing of private users. This was only pro forma, but when the newspapers blew it up out of all proportion, I was afraid the farmers would think that they were being discriminated against and that the law would make their tough job even tougher.

If I had been a member of Congress, I could have ducked the vote or passed off the responsibility to the committee which had drawn up the legislation—a committee made up mostly of representatives from "other" states. But as the Environmental Commissioner of Connecticut, I had no place to hide. On the day of the hearing, with a group of aroused farmers in attendance as well as all local media, I made sure I was the first one recognized by Representative Harlow, then Co-chairman of the Environmental Committee.

He called on me, saying, "Would you please state your name and your occupation."

"My name is Commissioner Dan Lufkin, from Newtown," I said, "and I'm a dairy farmer. I want to set the record straight and guarantee to you that farmers will not be adversely affected by this bill."

Just that close identification with their problems by one of their own number was enough to defuse the issue for the farmers and reassure them that the licensing in question would not complicate their lives or threaten their crops.

After the hearing, one of those humbling episodes took place which proves the immediacy of citizen interest in state government. As I stood in the hall of the Capitol, feeling somewhat self-satisfied over my appearance before the committee, a little old lady in white patent leather boots appeared. "You're a terrible Commissioner," she said.

Pointing to one of my administrative assistants, a charming and attractive young woman, she said, "Take the people you hire. Take this one, for instance. They're a dime a dozen. You should hire some older people who aren't young and attractive."

I said we had many unattractive people in the department, but she strolled off muttering, "I wish you would resign."

Although the example is an extreme one, rather than

being affronted by this exchange, I valued what it stood for. Right or wrong, here was a citizen who took the time, and had the opportunity, to dress down a commissioner for his personnel policies. This, to me, is the great and enduring strength of state government. When the people feel involved enough to confront *their* representatives in *their* state capitol, then state government must be very much alive indeed.

Because of my conviction that the generation to come is going to be, and indeed must be, one of increasing emphasis on government by, for and close to the people, I commissioned the Louis Harris Company, a nationally known polling organization, to sample public opinion about the states. Oddly enough, and symptomatic of our preoccupation with our federal establishment, no such survey had been conducted previously among a national cross-section. The results are not earth-shattering, but they are revealing. And they should give some comfort as well as warning to those who are planning to enter state and local politics, especially to those who plan to use such service as a stepping-stone to what they consider a more glorious career on the banks of the Potomac.

From questioning the public about their personal feelings toward centralized government, it seems clear that there has been a significant shift in the Washington-center-edness that characterized America from the 30s through the 60s.

In the generation which knew depression, world war, technological revolution and population growth, there seemed to be little that local governments could do to cope with such massive, world-shaking changes. Swollen with new powers, the federal bureaucracy was the undisputed engine of government. The states clattered after it, taking from it their speed, direction, and destination.

But, as the 1970s began, there were signs that the domination of the federal Establishment was beginning to subside. When Washington became increasingly preoccupied with foreign affairs, especially the prosecution of a divisive and unpopular war, the mystique of Washington's infallibility was irrevocably punctured. Even the glittering panaceas of Great Society domestic policy turned out to be only shiny shells, as even the best social programs buckled under inadequate funding, a too broad charter, and local opposition to "out-of-state" imposed solutions.

Because of disillusionment over government promises and distemper over bureaucratic indifference, the public began to search out other centers of effective political and social action. State and local governments were increasingly operating in the black and able to mount substantial programs of their own. The people, therefore, began to feel a renewed confidence in their ability to function—especially as the governorship and legislature began to attract a higher caliber of politician, instead of the time servers who had risen inexorably through the ranks of political hackdom or the penny-ante local business types who used state politics as an opportunity for economic back scratching. More than this, the public was also beginning to look with some favor toward the problem-solving capabilities of private enterprise after a generation in which business, especially big business, was anathema.

Monolithic dependence on Washington gave way to a more pluralistic response to the solution of problems. The people expressed a keen desire to conduct their social experiments closer to home and to try many different kinds of approaches. *By 3 to 1, the public felt that most of the Great Society programs of the 1960s had not worked out, and the reason given by most was "too much power concentrated in Washington."*

This does not mean that the people want the marble cake of Federalism to be sliced fifty ways, distributed equally to each of the fifty states with no share going to the federal government itself. We are not about to return to the weak national establishment envisioned in the original Articles of Confederation. As national crises in energy, urbanization, pollution, and population force us back upon ourselves, we are going to have to seek answers to our problems closer to home where accountability is on the line every day and your neighbor is making decisions which will affect him and his family as well as you and yours.

Because national and international news monopolizes the headlines and dominates the prime time news slots, there is an impression that people are totally ignorant of and bored with their state and local government. The opposite is true. According to our survey, *a very substantial 97 percent of the American people know where their state capitol is located* (see Table 1 in Appendix). *About half the population has visited the capitol, and observed at first hand the way in which state government is conducted* (Table 2). *A good third of the people have visited other offices of state government* (Tables 3 and 4), *and their ability to identify top state officials is surprisingly high, especially in relation to their ability to identify their national representatives.*

Compared with only 36 percent who know both U.S. senators from their state, 91 percent know the name of their governor, 81 percent are aware of his political affiliation, and 76 percent of those living in the largest one hundred and sixty cities in the country know the name of their mayor (Table 5).

It comes as something of a shock to realize that *only 58 percent know the name of even one of their senators, and individual congressmen are known to only 30 percent of their constituents,* indicating to me that representatives to the federal Congress are soon forgotten when they leave town and become "national" figures.

There is a relatively high degree of political sophistication among citizens of our states which most political commentators have either ignored or downplayed. *Half of all of them know which political party controls their state senate,* which is a highly significant factor in determining the outcome of elections (Table 6).

Even with emphasis shifting to state responsibility for the quality of life, *the overwhelming majority of Americans do not believe that their governors would make satisfactory presidents* (Table 7). There are probably many reasons for this, but two seem to prevail. Increasingly, the governor (president) of federal America requires great expertise in international affairs and in the complex process of national leadership, as opposed to local administration.

Once a state politician goes to Washington, especially as a senator, he becomes an overnight generalist in the national and international scene, losing his identity with the specific problems of his own home state. His political success is somewhat conditioned by his ability to please the home folks by his direct votes—witness former Senator Fulbright's dismal voting record on civil rights. But more often than not he is returned to office just because he has lost his provincialism and gained luster through his association with the great and glamorous names fed daily to the public through the media.

And so, the reasons why senators are preferred as presidential candidates are clustered around justifications like *"understands the national and international issues better,"* or *"has more understanding of the inner workings of federal government,"* or *"sees problems nationally not just for one state"* (Tables 8 and 9).

On the other hand, governors' qualifications are based on the assumption that *"running a whole state is like running the national government on a smaller scale,"* *"he knows the people's needs better because he has closer contact with them,"* and *"he knows more of the practical side of getting things done in government and politics"* (Tables 9 and 10).

It seems clear from this that the governor is prized for a "localness" which seems to weaken his desirability as a presidential candidate. The public wants a President it can revere at a distance. It prizes a governor for that very closeness which makes him better able to administer than to rule. At least in this case there's truth in the old definition of an expert as "anyone who's five hundred miles away."

For those governors and former governors who are quadriennial contestants among the front runners for the presidential nomination in 1976, the facts of this survey should be instructive. While one of them may, of course, be nominated, it seems likely that the popular predisposition to the Congress, especially the Senate, is not yet ready to be reversed. *There seems, in fact, rather weighty evidence that the public is not prepared to place the reins of national power in the hands of men who sit in the statehouse.* There is still a strong sense that governors are prized for their ability to deal with the more circumscribed problems of their states while federal leadership depends on an entirely different set of virtues, abilities and perspectives.

Even though there is a definite trend towards a pluralistic approach to government, *52 percent of the public chose the federal government when asked which level would most affect their daily lives over the next ten years. Only 19 percent felt that state government would have such a marked impact, and an equal number chose their local communities* (Table 11). The reasons for this, however, seem tied more to the facts of life in an inflationary and nuclear bomb-dominated world than to a desire to place responsibility for day-to-day decisions with the national bureaucracy. Almost every citizen knows that his life can be changed far more dramatically by decisions of war and peace, international economic policy, and world trade than by the more down-to-earth lawmaking that takes place in the statehouse.

When the question is rephrased to ask which level of government is more important in their daily lives, the state

*comes out in a dead heat with the federal establishment. The
addition of local government throws the emphasis sharply to
those centers of power closest to home* (Tables 12 and 13).
Clearly, while the people know that ultimate life or death
decisions are in the hands of their representatives in
Washington, they are just as aware that day-to-day
decisions, equally important in shaping individual destiny,
reside in the town halls and statehouse just down the road.

When asked what are the *"two or three most valuable
services your state government performs for its residents," the
large majority of state residents appear to have a solid
grounding in state accountability.* On a voluntary basis—
when no choices were given—*the largest number of people
mentioned education, followed by highways, public health,
police protection, law enforcement, welfare, parks and recreational facilities, and pollution control* (Table 14). All of these
have one essential thing in common. They impinge on
human existence on a direct, daily basis.

The popular conception of the role of the state, compared with the federal government, resembles the old joke
of the husband who said that *he* was allowed to make all
the big decisions, like should we recognize Red China or
send arms to Israel, while his wife made all the little
decisions, like where to live, what car to buy, how many
children to have and where the family vacation is taken.

*When people were asked what the federal government's
major services should be, they were listed as national defense,
social security, cancer research, and drug reform—all of
which can have a devastating long-range impact on the
society—the big decisions.*

When they were given a shopping list of services and
asked to say where key decisions should be made, the state
and its subdivisions were given clear priority in four basic
areas, all of which directly influence the quality of daily
life—the little decisions. These are, as I have discussed in

the previous chapter, education by a 72 percent to 23 percent margin; transportation 62 percent to 29 percent; welfare 56 percent to 39 percent, and housing 65 percent to 28 percent. Prison reform, drug reform, and pollution control are close, but clearly most people do not feel that these areas of policy or of lawmaking affect them as directly. Therefore, on balance, they would just as soon assign them to the federal government as to the state government (Table 15).

Ultimately then, *the only areas in which federal dominion really is decisive in the public view are national defense, Social Security, and cancer research.* This is the clearest indication yet that the state and local governments are regarded by the people as crucial to maintaining the quality of life most Americans desire.

There seems to be considerable sophistication, too, concerning the question of paying for these desired services. Federal revenue sharing is an idea which has definitely penetrated the public consciousness. *In an era of soaring costs and rising taxes, the public wants to see the burden of payment shared with the federal government but with the control of expenditures and the administration of programs closer at hand where they can be observed and evaluated.*

When asked where revenue sharing dollars should be spent by the states, education retains its place as the Number One priority for local action. Health is second in importance (Table 16). For even though government health insurance, health maintenance, and national research programs are seen primarily as federal concerns, the public wants to see local health facilities which affect their lives most directly given the assistance of federal revenue sharing dollars. Programs for the poor are a surprising third. Even though widespread disaffection with the so-called War on Poverty programs has been recorded, Louis Harris and other observers report that public concern for the poor is once again rising, despite an uneasy concern with rising welfare costs.

Here, too, quality of life seems to be a decisive element. Throughout all segments of society, there appears to run a basic sentiment that as long as there is economic injustice accorded the few, the many cannot properly enjoy life's abundance. *Seventy-six percent of all Americans believe that government at all levels has a fundamental responsibility for the poor and a substantial percentage of these are willing to see revenue sharing dollars go toward redressing social and economic inequities.*

Transportation, which is perceived as a priority service of the state, is rated low on the value scale of revenue sharing. There seems to be a growing awareness, stimulated both by the energy crisis and the environmental crusade that more and better highways are not the answer to a higher quality of life. While there is no parallel rise of interest in mass transportation, the American people seem to regard massive highway construction as a relic of a more prodigal past. *At least, Americans do not want their states to waste revenue sharing funds on getting them where they want to go. Instead, they want these dollars to be concentrated on services that will improve life where they are.*

One serious obstacle to the success of revenue sharing, which probably is due to its newness, *lies in the majority opinion that these dollars could be spent to better advantage in reducing state taxes than in improving and expanding state services* (Table 17). Clearly, if the states decide to use revenue sharing solely to reduce state taxes instead of creatively using it to satisfy human needs, the intent of this highly promising program will be frustrated from the start.

On this issue, the survey indicates the line-up for and against change in American society. *The most affluent, the best educated, the younger people, and the minorities form an active though no longer explosive coalition for change.*

Aligned against them is a grouping of Americans centered largely in the suburbs, made up primarily of older citizens, the least educated, and those with incomes under fifteen thousand dollars. If the states will assume the degree of leadership that the constituency for change commands of them, the battle of revenue sharing for sound programs as well as tax reduction can be won. Yet, this could become a bitterly contested issue as revenue sharing grows in size and becomes more deeply embedded in the normal processes of government.

On the question of taxation itself, the public clearly believes that at the federal level the graduated income tax is the fairest form of taxation. Property taxes rate a strong second, but almost no one believes that the federal government has any right to levy on locally based private property which is already staggering under the weight of local tax burdens (Table 18).

On the state level, the sales tax is perceived as the fairest tax, followed not too closely by an income tax, with a state property tax—even for education—limping well in the rear (Table 19). On a comparative basis, it seems clear that the appetite for further sales taxes seems to be subsiding while the unpopularity of the state income tax continues even though over forty states have currently enacted such a tax. *On the local level, the sales tax is well in the lead, yet property taxes account for the largest proportion of local revenues by far.*

The increasing respect for state and local government evidenced in this public opinion survey is greatly encouraging to anyone who believes that the "Dynamic States" constitute the action edge of American politics over the next generation. For too long, we have invested in a relative handful of career politicians and entrenched bureaucrats all our hopes and expectations for a better life and a peaceful world. It is time we gave more than lip service to home rule and made our local levels of government even more responsive to and responsible for our desires for the kind of life we want to live where we have to live it.

But there's a dark thread running through every response. It is the deep and underlying cynicism which, at this time at least, is directed primarily at the federal government which in the early 1970s seems to have earned Robert Allen's epithet of "the bawdy house of politics."

Fifty-two percent of the American people of every political leaning and social, educational, and income level believe that corruption at the federal level is "very serious." Add another 29 percent who feel it is "somewhat serious," and we find that more than 80 percent of all Americans look upon their national leadership with a jaded, distrustful eye (Table 20).

Significantly lower percentages feel that corruption is rife in state and local government even though a majority of our citizens characterizes government, at every level, as corrupt.

The extent to which faith in the federal establishment has been eroded can be seen most dramatically when the question is phrased, "Which one level of government has the most corruption?" Then the federal government leads the way, at 54 percent, followed distantly by state government at 17 percent and local government at 14 percent (Table 21).

There is obviously a desperate need to repair the damage of Watergate and related incidents and to raise the public respect for our great national democracy. If we succumb to cynicism over national politics, we do not strengthen our ability to be governed at the state and local level but poison the entire system. For too long we have believed the myth that government must be corrupt because all power corrupts, that politics cannot exist without the mutual handwashing and influence-peddling that have seemed indispensable to getting things done in an otherwise slow and bungling democracy.

But government does not have to depend on favoritism, bribery, or illegal activities. It functions well when it is placed in the open marketplace of public scrutiny and removed from the back rooms of private dealings and secret arrangements. Only when there is no place to hide do the governed and the governing meet at the same table and deal with the same agenda. Only when tough and inviolable legislation rigidly enforced removes the profitability from public-private collusion will our cynicism prove to be groundless and our system become healthy once more.

The people are not fooled even by those actions and alliances conducted in the deepest secrecy. *When asked the degree of influence they feel the private sector has on government at all levels, they rank large corporations, financial institutions, and organized labor one, two, three, with the greatest amount of influence felt at the federal level. Sadly, only a pitiful handful rate the influence of the average citizen as meaningful at any level of government. But, as might be expected, they believe that what influence the citizen has increases as government moves closer to him. Most shocking of all, organized crime is thought to have a great deal of influence at all levels but most of all at the federal level* (Tables 22 and 23).

It is too early to say whether this public awareness is accompanied by indignation. But the place to begin the cure is at those levels of government which can be most closely examined and most clearly perceived. At the state level there is a great dual challenge to prove that effective administration need not be corrupt and to demonstrate that good government can enhance quality of life for all.

The people are not fools, and in our democracy they possess a weapon more powerful than money or influence —the vote. I suppose a small percentage of voters and politicians alike will always be available for hire. But it is the uncorruptible majority of people in the streets, on the farms, and in the factories who count most when the votes are being tallied.

As long as the people have the freedom to express their admiration or distaste for how they are being served, America does not have to fear. The more the administration of policies and programs is brought down to the state and local level, the better the people will be able to judge who is fair, who is honest, who is creative, and who is productive and efficient. And once they are adept at discerning these qualities in the people they appoint to govern them close to home, the voters will become increasingly difficult to deceive at the national level.

By strengthening the effectiveness of state government, we strengthen the entire federal system, for, as Daniel Elazar rightly says, "State governments are the keystones of the American governmental arch." [39]

As long as these "50 keystones" are strongly in place, the arch may teeter at the top or wobble at the bottom, but it will stand. And in a world of abrupt and violent change, there is much to be said for that.

CHAPTER 10

Summing Up

★

Having served as Connecticut's first Commissioner of Environmental Protection for two years, I was beginning to realize that there is a time for leaving government service as well as a time for entering it. Much of what we had set out to do had been accomplished. We had come a long way from Public Act 872, the few faces, the few volunteers, and the cavernous Room #539 we started with. Even the wonderful, vivacious Marlene Bakewell, who had started with me back in the first days of the department and who was the very effective "Executive Secretary and Scorekeeper," was beginning to frown more often—and that I knew was meaningful.

There were no miracles, but in a hundred small ways it was evident that Connecticut's long slide to environmental degradation had been reversed. A young, aggressive department was in place. The legislature had given us all the power we could carefully handle and then some. In air and water pollution control, protection of wetlands, solid waste management, and overall environmental enforcement we had been granted unparalleled authority. The governor had never wavered in his support, and if Finance Commissioner Adolf Carlson had not been converted, at least he was not trying to convert me anymore.

The period of peak legislative activity, public evangelism and administrative reorganization had ended. In Douglas Costle and Ted Bampton, my deputies, the state had strong, experienced administrators dedicated to the citizen's welfare who could build solidly on the foundation we had laid. Now, I felt, I wanted to step back for a while to view what we had done from a perspective of time and distance. To try to generalize on the lessons I had learned during this incomparable experience of state service.

Compared with the inflated rhetoric we were used to receiving from Washington, our accomplishments were modest and tentative. But there were measurable results. No one had been deceived by excessive claims or disappointed by grandiose promises. We had not guaranteed to build a new Jerusalem on Connecticut's "green and pleasant land." We had not poured huge sums of money into research or demonstration projects that could never be duplicated or expanded. And, above all, we had not vacated the premises when things got tough.

If the citizens had complaints, they knew where to find us. If there was a factory in violation, or a wetland being illegally filled, or a vandal defacing a state park, the complaint could be made to a responsible local authority. If performance was unsatisfactory, a number of alternatives were available. A town neighbor in the legislature could be called. A local political leader could be informed. If all else failed—or even before anything else was tried—the commissioner's telephone number was public property. As Elise, my wife, can verify, all too well, I was on call day or night, and generally able to set things in motion even if I couldn't guarantee total satisfaction.

Perhaps I was naive when I joined state government. I really believed that our obligation to the people should increase in direct proportion to our proximity to them. This was a revolutionary concept to some of the more seasoned bureaucrats in the older agencies which had been melded into the Department of Environmental Protection.

Shortly after I took office, I called together the department heads and made a very simple request. Passing around copies of a letter I had just sent out to a citizen, I said, "Do you understand what I've written at the end of the letter?" They all scanned the paper carefully and nodded their heads. "What does it mean?" I asked.

"Well," said one, "it's your way of closing the letter. Like 'sincerely yours.' "

"Look again," I said. "It says, *'At your service.'* That's more than a closing—it's a beginning, and it's the way I want every letter coming out of this office to end. But more than that, I want you to mean it and live it."

Several of my department heads looked at me in complete amazement. Their idea of service had been to go by the book. They served their commissioner, and he the governor who had appointed him. That is the way the bureaucracy worked. The public? Who were they?

"That's going to take a lot of time from our 'regular' work," said one. "We'll have to put on more staff."

"No," I said, "I want *you* to be of service, not your staff. That's the reason we're here—the only reason—that *is* our 'regular' work."

And that's the way we tried to operate throughout my tenure as commissioner.

There is just no way a congressman, senator, or federal civil servant can say, "At your service" to a local citizen and really mean it. There are too many layers of authority to penetrate before a question can be answered, much less acted upon. And, if the request or complaint has to do with a local problem, it must be bucked back to the state with all the attendant delays and opportunities for error, forgetfulness, or deliberate avoidance. If the Department of Environmental Protection accomplished nothing else during my two years as its commissioner, it did become responsive to the people. This responsiveness, I believe, is the first and most important justification for state and local government.

As I was struggling with my conscience and my

judgment, deciding whether or when I should leave office, I heard something that helped tip the scales. One of the department's field inspectors had been taking some samples of the Naugatuck River below Waterbury. As he worked, he struck up a conversation with an old man who had lived near the river most of his life. "You know," the old man said, "the grass has come back on the river bank for the first time in years. Must be a sign that the water is getting cleaner."

I took this as a sign, as well, that the most important things I could accomplish in this job were now behind me. It was not very dramatic evidence of success. Just a few blades of new grass on a much used river bank. But to me it was an unmistakable omen that the work, the sacrifice, the hearings and the legislation, the money and the manpower, all those phone calls and the letters signed "At your service" were coming together at last. Finally, when Ted Bampton gave the order which stocked trout in the Willimantic River for the first time in ten years, I felt confident that Connecticut was at last moving purposefully in the direction of environmental preservation rather than drifting unconsciously toward environmental ruin.

Beyond the grass on the banks of the Naugatuck and trout in the Willimantic, the government and the people of the sovereign state of Connecticut had demonstrated their will and ability to take action to protect the environment of their five thousand square miles of America. No other political entity could have done it for them. Not regionally. Not nationally. The results came because the people themselves had a special feeling for that particular cube of land, air and water which had been entrusted to them. Connecticut's political leadership had been willing to act firmly in cracking down on environmental degradation, and Connecticut's industry had demonstrated the statesmanship to participate.

And so, Connecticut's ambient air showed a 50 percent

reduction in sulphur dioxide within a year after the Clean Air Standards were established. Because of the national energy crisis, there may be some slippage in these levels, but the DEP has demonstrated no inclination to surrender its hard-won standards to industry and utility pressure to burn coal and higher sulphur content fuel indefinitely.

In the national panic to sacrifice long-term environmental considerations to the short-term energy crisis, Connecticut is maintaining both its standards and its integrity. As *The Hartford Courant* wrote in an editorial in the depths of a frigid December, "The energy crunch could benefit the environment. Gasoline restrictions will mean less driving and so less air pollution. Heating oil reductions will dictate better home insulation and more energy-conscious architecture. Critical looks at American energy consumption will encourage more recycling. Altogether, the energy conservation ethic could broaden general awareness of scarcity and the need for careful husbanding of earth's resources. The urban renaissance could get a boost as people realize the cities' basic efficiency for work, shopping, entertainment."

To me, this wise and moderate statement characterizes the responsibility Connecticut people have shown to their state and to each other. No proclamation from Washington could have produced such a determined effort to turn hardship into opportunity.

Long before the energy shortage reached critical proportions, the government of Connecticut, reflecting the will and character of its people, had passed the laws and set in place the mechanisms needed to protect the state against most ecological eventualities. The new Resources Recovery System to handle the state's garbage should enhance the state's energy supply by producing a very low-sulphur-content fuel which could eventually provide up to 15 percent of the state's electrical needs. Even with a lowering of fuel quality standards, most Connecticut

industries will not pollute air or water because they have
already completed their pollution control installations—
impelled by strict laws and encouraged by generous
incentives and financial arrangements provided by the
state and federal government.

After resigning as Commissioner of Environmental
Protection, I spent time reflecting on the lessons I had
learned in state service. I ranched in Grant County,
Oregon, which is roughly the same size as Connecticut yet
has only eight thousand inhabitants—much as Connecticut's population must have been when the English first
arrived here in the seventeenth century.

But unlike Connecticut, which for three hundred years
has encouraged unplanned and unlimited industrial development and random population growth until it has
achieved a concentration of six hundred people per square
mile, the third most densely populated state in the Union,
the citizens of Grant County have determined to regulate
growth and to plan expansion. They have adopted a
land-use program not only to maintain the county's
character as an agricultural and ranching community but
to guarantee land use which will be consistent with the
land's productivity and long-term ability to sustain life. In
short, the burden of proof is placed on any potential
developer to demonstrate that any development planned is
in harmony and not in conflict with the character and
desires of the community.

The people of Grant County, adopting the tone and
philosophy set by the leadership of their state, know that
without planning and regulation on a local level, their land
will become subject to statewide or federal planning. Or,
what is worse, to the planning or no planning of private
developers and overflow populations. They've seen that
scenario played out by their neighbors to the south—the
once golden paradise of California.

In Grant County, they know full well that random

growth will totally destroy the agricultural potential of the land and wreck its current economy and character. They know that the bulldozing of forests and ridge lines will permit flooding and degrade water quality, as will the filling of wetland areas. They know that building small-lot communities will pollute the water, and new highway and access routes will bring trucks and automobiles in sufficient numbers to degrade the air, and drive away the wildlife they cherish and the life they love.

Even if Grant County had not decided to plan its future development, it would probably have never become another Connecticut. Rail and water transportation, accessibility to major markets, concentrations of highways, rail lines, existing industry, and a large labor force are all absent and may never become available. And even if Grant County could become a Connecticut in a generation or a century, it seems to me that the citizens who hold that land in trust should be able to make such a decision of their own free will, just as long as it does not violate national policy or federal law.

This is the vital asset management role which must remain firmly in the hands of the state and local governments where the land is located. The land-hungry speculators of the East and West coasts might not be able to understand the attitudes of a Grant County. But the governments of these states and their political subdivisions can.

Land-use planning is the next essential agenda item for the fifty states—with firm and constructive guidelines coming from Washington. No all-encompassing, national land-use planning program will satisfy the needs of Connecticut and Oregon alike. Each must be permitted to put its own unique stamp on any planning within its sovereign borders. As with race, housing, and environment, we need a clear statement of national policy and national direction, but within such a context, the states must be free to represent and execute the flexible and diverse wishes, goals, and expectations of their citizens.

When it does have direct control of the land, I have found that the federal government is often too concerned with politics on the national level to administer firmly for the benefit of the land and those who are most immediately affected by it.

In Oregon, I discovered that while the federal government is quite strict in its protection of public lands against the depredations of cattle and timber interests, it does not have the courage and the local concern to provide similar protection against large numbers of citizens who represent substantial votes. And so the beautiful Strawberry Mountain National Forest in eastern Oregon, a federal preserve, is being systematically destroyed by hordes of hikers, campers, trail-bike riders, and various and sundry groups because the federal government doesn't have the stomach or the good sense to regulate usage in line with the capabilities of the land to support such usage.

If this natural paradise were controlled by local interests, there might be an equal disregard of environmental consideration in the name of development for increased property tax revenue or for private profit. But at least there would be some pressure points on which citizens might apply influence—a neighbor with a conscience to appeal to, a local zoning board or environmental agency which would listen. But because the federal authority is an absentee landlord, there is little hope of ever getting a hearing. I know. I tried. And so, Strawberry Mountain in ten or twenty years will no longer be fit for camping and recreation. Not because the people are willfully destructive but because no system of granting licenses or permits is in place to balance land use with the ability of the land to handle it.

In such a situation, there is everywhere to hide, with no one on the scene to be held accountable. Chalk up another point for the states. If Strawberry Mountain had been in Connecticut as part of its park and forest system, the Department of Environmental Protection would long since have imposed the few simple land-use restrictions necessary to keep the land alive, beautiful, and available for the people to use and enjoy for generations to come.

This seems to be yet another reason for rethinking the role of the federal and state governments in managing assets and handling problems within state borders. If there is indeed to be a reshifting of responsibility and a sincerely motivated reallocation of funds from Washington to the states, some of the anomalies which have developed historically should be removed. The states should be given a larger role in controlling the physical resources within their borders, sharing management responsibility with the federal government for those immense tracts which cross state boundaries and are designated as "national resource lands."

Just as there is no reason why a federal agency should permit a state land resource to be destroyed, there is no reason why a federal agency without any effective input from the state should be able to grant timber, grazing, mineral, or other development rights to private corporations. The state should have a major role in determining what happens to its physical assets, always, of course, within broad national policy guidelines. Yet in vast areas of our country these decisions are being made in private by government agencies which have little knowledge of or interest in the long-range needs, plans and programs of the states.

When it comes to the management of human resources, I believe the responsibility should be reversed. Recent polls indicate that the people of the United States agree. In the *Survey of Public Attitudes* commissioned from the Louis Harris organization by the Senate Committee on Government Operations, an overwhelming 89 percent of the American public records its belief that "the federal government has a deep responsibility for seeing to it that the poor are taken care of, that no one goes hungry, and that every person achieves a minimum standard of living." This would seem to prove that the people are not opposed to federal support of those programs which guarantee minimum material standards. It was wholly logical, then, for the federal government to accept primary responsibility for all programs involving basic living standards for the disabled, blind, and elderly under new welfare legislation.

Relieved of the crushing burden of welfare, the states should be able to concentrate on what I believe should be their primary responsibilities—the management of all physical resources, i.e., water, land, air, forests, parks, minerals—within their boundaries. Federal departments now managing significant land areas and negotiating their use or exploitation without the consent of the state should serve primarily in a consultive capacity when the interests of more than one state are involved. They may also serve as conduits of financial assistance through revenue sharing to augment the state's fiscal resources in making efficient asset management possible.

In a book entitled *A Thirty-eight State U.S.A.*, Professor G. Etzel Pearcy, who teaches geography at California State College in Los Angeles, proposes that state lines be redrawn, creating a country of thirty-eight new states which would be more equal as to size, population and resources. He estimates that such a grouping would save about $4.6 billion in the cost of state government alone. For one thing, he would create new states with major metropolitan areas at their core. His new state of Hudson, for example, would include parts of New Jersey, Connecticut, Massachusetts, Pennsylvania and southern New York with New York City as its center. Chicago would be the hub of the new state of Dearborn. Alaska, which the professor points out is four hundred eighty-three times bigger than Rhode Island, would be divided into Seward and Kodiak.

Such schemes based on equalization of size and resources are interesting exercises in nation building, but they miss an entire meaning of the states which transcends cost and even efficiency of government. Although it is impossible to rationalize present state size or boundaries, these have become facts embedded in our national history. They give our society much of its incredible diversity. Despite the sameness of architecture and commerce which tends to make every main street and shopping center in America look alike, there are still large and exciting differences in life-style among the states. To a great extent, our people are still free to choose what suits them best; to take on the characteristics of that state in which they live—or to move on if the ambience of a region does not please them, whether because of climate, urbanization, opportunity, or pace of change.

It is a fact that no matter how many states there are or how large or small they may be, the states are essential to the preservation of our political, economic and social system. To a degree, we have arrived at our present mood of national disillusionment and disarray not because the states play too great a part in our lives but because the federal government has given them too little to do.

The Government Operations Committee survey indicates dramatically that while confidence in every layer of government has declined in the past four or five years, the greatest loss of faith has been in the ability of Washington to deliver on its promises. Fifty-seven percent of all Americans have less confidence in the national government while only 26 percent have experienced a similar reaction toward the states.

It is on the somewhat shaky foundation of this residual good will that we must begin to build a new kind of Federalism. For whether or not the states are the right size or shape, they and their subdivisions are where three-quarters of the American people want to see power concentrated. As the Harris survey points out, 74 percent of the public recognizes that each state has "different people with different needs" that cannot be well served by national programs dispensed wholesale from Washington. They overwhelmingly prefer to have the states initiate and operate government programs.

They feel instinctively that local government, being closer to the needs of the people, should handle most services required by the people. They agree that elected officials have lost control over the great national bureaucracies. And they conclude that "the federal government has become so big and bureaucratic that it should give more money and power to the states and local communities." This is one of the most striking revelations ever provided by the American people of their attitudes toward the federal system.

Every political party has been searching for a "New Majority" on which to build a coalition which will assure its maintenance of national political power. The Democrats, for a generation, built their political hegemony on a base of organized labor, the cities, the South, and racial and ethnic minorities. The Nixon administration thought it had been given a mandate by heartland farmers, suburbanites, and the new blue-collar middle class.

If I interpret this survey correctly, the parties have been wrong. The "New Majority" was drawn to the Republicans in 1968 and again in 1972 not because of strict constitutional constructionism, or emphasis on law and order, or the implied promise of a slowdown in racial integration. True, these may have caused some voters to switch from traditional political alliances. Basically, however, I believe the overwhelming mandate given former President Richard Nixon in 1972 was a mandate to share power with the people. The citizens at home want regulation and administration located where they can see it and control it rather than in the federal bureaucracy, even if that power is used to promote programs at least on the surface pleasing to them. But instead of receiving more power at the state level, the people have been treated thus far to a bitter struggle for national power between the executive branch and the Congress. This in part is what Watergate was really all about. An imperial presidency was being challenged by a frustrated, national Congress which had watched its power being eroded. And in the process the real interests of the people and a stronger role for the states are being almost totally submerged if not abandoned.

When the mayors of America gathered at the 1973 Conference of the National League of Cities, they roundly criticized the "New Federalism" as "a mandate from the White House to accept its definition of an orderly process of government." They were treated to the sentiments of a member of the House of Representatives, Thomas L. Ashley of Ohio, who branded the New Federalism and its revenue sharing program as "aggrandizement of power in the White House at the expense of Congress."

The people have become impatient with this kind of pulling and hauling at the federal level, which they already thoroughly distrust. They do not accept members of the House and Senate as being truly representative of their local interests. They want power shared directly through their local governments, not through congressional inter-mediaries who are just as remote, just as difficult to reach, as the walled-in bureaucracy of the executive branch.

As Theodore White points out in *The Making of the President—1972*, "The underlying reality of American politics is that central national power is just as highly valued by the committees and subcommittees of Congress as it is by the executive departments." [40]

And so I think there is compelling evidence for a new

national alignment based on the localization of power. No
candidate or political party expecting to win future
elections can ignore this popular demand for an end to
secrecy, an end to exclusion, an end to imperial power
whether it is concentrated in the executive branch or the
houses of Congress. But nothing is going to happen to
make the "New Federalism" work until the states have a
greater role in shaping the policies that will bring about
the redistribution of power. If left to Congress and the
executive branch, "New Federalism" will remain an empty
slogan—power will never leave Washington.

To advise on the administration of "New Federalism"
programs, and to make certain that the voice of the states
is not excluded from national policy-making, one of the
nation's governors, perhaps the elected chairman of the
Governor's Conference, should be given Cabinet rank and
invited to participate in the federal process of domestic
program development. I realize that one individual from
the ranks of state government is no match for the legions
of the legislative and executive branches. But simply
because he *is* one man speaking and listening for the states
he would have unique stature and prestige. More than any
congressman or senator, he would symbolize a determination to restore power and authority to that level of
government closest to the people. As it stands now, the
federal government has little capacity to deal with governors or even former governors on the national level.
Several excellent governors were appointed to Cabinet
positions in the first Nixon administration. Romney,
Hickel, and Volpe tried earnestly to square their firsthand
knowledge of the immediacy and urgency of public need
with their remote and essentially powerless administrative
roles. The results were inevitably unhappy, as was Governor Love's brief adventure as the former President's first
energy czar.

In previous administrations, former governors have

been similarly frustrated and impotent. Hopefully, a governor with Cabinet status *as* a governor, representing the states, would find that role more compatible with his political philosophy and responsibilities. At the very least, the other 49 governors would have a true friend in court. No longer would they have to rely on the annual presidential or vice-presidential appearances at their Governors' Conference to find out at first hand how the administration is planning to deal with the problems of the states. The fact that a viable two-party system now exists in every state would preclude the possibility of the "national governor" becoming a captive of the party in power. Beyond politics he would be the advocate of the states—filling the void that clearly exists. For while the people are demanding a greater share in power and responsibility for the states, the states themselves are almost without representation in Washington. And this is a situation which must be remedied if the public will is to prevail.

In his book, *The Party's Over*, David Broder states a fundamental thesis, that the existence of two viable and healthy parties is essential to the strength and survival of our political system. Though I agree with this premise, I do not think it goes far enough. The smugness, the complacency, the apathy and insensitivity he ascribes to the disintegration of our two-party system have been caused at least in equal part by the centralization of power in Washington and the struggle between Congress and the President—a struggle not to represent the people, but to possess a truly impregnable national power base.

What has gone wrong with us transcends party and partisanship. In the concentration of power in Washington, we have neglected the true source of our political strength, the representative quality of our Republic which is not only of, by and for the people, but close enough to them so that there is no place to hide.

Broder says, "I do not expect to see again in America
the kind of smugness, of euphoria that gripped Washington when I came to the capital city sixteen years ago. Since
then, we have gone through the New Frontier, the Great
Society and the New American Revolution, each briefer in
duration and more patently false in its promise than the
slogan that preceded it. If there is one thing the long
travail of the last four presidencies has taught us, it is to be
skeptical of the easy answer." [41]

But pinning great hopes on the revitalization of our
political parties is itself too easy an answer. As long as our
parties are held in thrall by the vision of imperial power,
we are going to be saddled by the same false promises and
shabby hand-me-down programs we have known for more
than a generation. Certainly the give and take of political
differences, and the vitality of partisan contests contribute
to our capacity to test various political ideas and make
choices between men and philosophies. When *any* party
wins control of the White House, it becomes bemused by
the toys and gadgets of power. It forgets the diversity of
the nation which installed it in office and seeks a
permanent, homogenized constituency on which it can
rely for everlasting re-election.

We will not be restored as a democratic society until we
have reenergized the fundamental basis of our federal
system. This means returning to the people—through their
state and local representatives—the power to make independent local decisions within the broad framework of
national policy. It also means providing funds in significant amounts to permit local government to function
creatively and in the best interests of those it serves—to
deal with the people as neighbors, not as subjects.

Flying across this continent, one becomes aware that
town, county and state boundaries are only imaginary
lines of demarcation. Beneath the windows of the airplane
the continent unfolds not as a map but as a single mass of

land, mountains flowing into plains and prairies, rivers and roads dividing the land instead of the familiar state borders that decorate our maps. And yet, there is always the presence of local government totally attuned to the lives of the people living within its arbitrary, imaginary boundaries—the network of state legislators, town officials, county agents, mayors, selectmen, police, fire fighters, commissioners, state office holders, all poignantly aware of the immediate concerns of that piece of geography for which they share responsibility.

When the energy crisis came upon us, these men and women were not bickering over broad national policy but trying to figure out how best to heat the homes of their people, how to conserve their fuel, how to compromise between environmental concerns and the need for more heat and power for their citizens. While Congress was still arguing over a national energy bill, Tom Meskill in Connecticut was slapping a 50-mile-an-hour speed limit on all highways within the state, going on television to urge the people to turn back their thermostats to 68 degrees, ordering a halt on all unnecessary state travel and calling upon all Connecticut residents to prepare to share and to sacrifice over the coming hard, cold winter.

While Washington bureaucrats were arguing interminably about how far to go in relaxing environmental standards, Doug Costle and Chris Beck of the Department of Environmental Protection were grappling with the real issues of whether to permit the utility companies to burn coal or higher sulphur-content fuel oil and telling them they could be granted a temporary exception only if they installed adequate treatment in their stacks. Hundreds of boards and commissions, citizen groups and legislative committees were meeting in all the towns and cities of America, each in its own way attempting to serve the diverse needs and the conflicting interests of the people *where they live.*

As I returned to Connecticut, again as a private citizen, I found my conviction reinforced that down there in the small towns and crowded cities, the town halls, and the state office buildings is where the real social and political history of America is being written. To be useful to his state is as broad an ambition as an American need possess, for in serving the people of his state he is best serving the interests of the nation as a whole.

Not that everyone agrees. Max Frankel, in an article in the *New York Times Magazine*, detailed all that is supposedly wrong with local government in a frontal assault on the basic premises of revenue sharing:

"Whoever presumes to talk of invigorating these local governments and their state counterparts is talking about many governors condemned to serve one brief term. He is talking about state legislatures, a number of which still meet only in alternate years, and most of which are ill paid, ill staffed, and ill housed. He is talking about multiple systems of state justice in which judges are often subject to partisan election without regard for their professional qualifications. He is talking about mayors, managers, executives, school boards, directors, commissioners, assessors, and the Lord knows who else with wholly uncoordinated mandates, all scrambling for taxes and loans and subsidies and carrying out their own areas of sovereignty and authority." [42]

That is a typical view of the states from the lofty perspective of Washington, where the teeming variety of American life becomes reduced to the activities of about five hundred men and women in Congress and several hundred thousand bureaucrats who are insulated from the vigorous, often violent, real world they are supposed to represent.

Although I tended to accept Frankel's stereotype before I became a part of state government, it shattered and dissolved as I became increasingly familiar with the reality which underlay the cliché. During my two years as Commissioner of Environmental Protection, I found my faith strengthened and my ideals nourished by the devotion, effort and compassionate intelligence I met at every level of state and local government. Through three sessions of the state legislature, through the difficult days of starting up a totally new administrative entity, through a bus strike and an energy crisis, through a business recession and an erosion of confidence in a courageous governor doing his honest best for the state, I found myself constantly surprised by the fresh and willing spirit of the people and their local representatives.

That spirit is symbolized by a brief but poignant encounter which took place shortly after I became Commissioner. Almost as soon as the department was organized, we received a letter from a little girl who was desperately concerned about the survival of a family of ospreys which came each year to their nesting grounds at Lake Wononscopomic, in northwestern Connecticut, near her home. She wanted to know what we were doing to protect these beautiful birds so they would always return to a safe habitat in Connecticut. Instead of responding with form letter number 287, or what is typical of our federal bureaucracy, not answering her at all, we invited her to our office and outlined our efforts to preserve the osprey.

As we said good-bye, she looked me in the eye—drew herself up to her full forty-eight inches and said, "If anything happens to my osprey, I'll know who's to blame."

That told me everything I needed to know about state government. No airy promises. No passing the buck. No place to hide.

Now, even though I am no longer commissioner, I worry about the safety of that osprey. For if anything should happen, I am certain my phone will ring some night and an irate ten-year-old will ask, "Well? What do you have to say now?"

No place to hide. That's the way the people want their government to work at every level. If we are to survive as a decent and honorable nation effectively serving the needs of our people at home, that is the kind of government the people must be given.

APPENDIX

A Study of the American People's
Attitudes Toward State Government
in the 1970s

Conducted by
LOUIS HARRIS AND ASSOCIATES, INC.

TABLE 1

KNOWLEDGE OF WHAT CITY THE STATE CAPITOL IS IN

	Know Correctly %	Don't Know %
Total	97	3
East	96	4
Midwest	98	2
South	95	5
West	98	2
Black	90	10
White	97	3

TABLE 2

HAVE YOU EVER VISITED THE STATE CAPITOL BUILDING?

	Have Visited %	Have Not Visited %	Not Sure %
Total	49	51	*
East	42	57	1
Midwest	57	43	*
South	50	50	*
West	49	51	—
18–29	47	53	*
30–49	48	52	*
50 and over	52	47	1
8th grade	37	63	*
High school	46	54	*
College	61	38	1
Under $5,000	42	58	—
$5,000–$9,999	48	52	*
$10,000–$14,999	53	46	1
$15,000 and over	56	44	—
Black	34	66	*
White	52	48	*

TABLE 3

HAVE YOU EVER VISITED AN OFFICE OF THE STATE
GOVERNMENT IN THE STATE CAPITAL OR
SOMEWHERE ELSE IN THE STATE?

	Have Visited %	*Have Not Visited* %	*Not Sure* %
Total	33	66	1
East	26	73	1
Midwest	41	59	*
South	33	66	1
West	34	66	*
8th grade	18	81	1
High school	29	71	*
College	47	52	1
Under $5,000	25	75	—
$5,000–$9,999	30	69	1
$10,000–$14,999	36	63	1
$15,000 and over	42	58	*
Black	18	82	—
White	35	64	1

TABLE 4

WHEN DID YOU LAST VISIT AN OFFICE
OF THE STATE GOVERNMENT?

	Total %
Have not visited	66
Within the last month	3
1–6 months ago	4
7–12 months ago	3
1–5 years ago	13
More than 5 years ago	10
Not sure	1
Median	2.2 years ago

TABLE 5

FAMILIARITY WITH GOVERNMENT OFFICIALS

	Total %	East %	Midwest %	South %	West %	Cities %	Suburbs %	Towns %	Rural %	18-29 %	30-49 %	50 and Over %	8th Grade %	High School %	College %	Under $5,000 %	$5,000-$9,999 %	$10,000-$14,999 %	$15,000 and Over %	Black %	White %
Your Governor																					
Know correctly	91	95	92	84	94					86	93	94	85	89	98	86	88	94	97	71	94
Don't know	9	5	8	16	6					14	7	6	15	11	2	14	12	6	3	29	6
Senator From Your State																					
Know correctly	58	55	60	57	65					54	60	61	43	54	74	50	54	64	72	40	61
Don't know	42	45	40	43	35					46	40	39	57	46	26	50	46	36	28	60	39
Second Senator From Your State																					
Know correctly	36	33	40	31	44					30	37	40	23	30	52	27	33	39	50	13	39
Don't know	64	67	60	69	56					70	63	60	77	70	48	73	67	61	50	87	61
Your Congressman																					
Know correctly	38	29	44	44	33	50	28	34	34	31	42	40	25	35	48	31	32	40	52	68	80
Don't know	62	71	56	56	67	50	72	66	66	69	58	60	75	65	52	69	68	60	48	32	20
Your Mayor*																					
Know correctly	76	88	82	74	58	87	43			74	74	80	71	78	76	70	75	80	76	69	79
Don't know	24	12	18	26	42	13	57			26	26	20	29	22	24	30	25	20	24	31	21

* Base: Only if live in largest 160 cities in U.S. = 35%

TABLE 6

KNOWLEDGE OF WHAT POLITICAL PARTY CONTROLS
THE STATE SENATE IN YOUR STATE

	Know Correctly %	Don't Know %
Total	48	52
East	44	56
Midwest	48	52
South	53	47
West	48	52
18–29	41	59
30–49	48	52
50 and over	54	46
8th grade	40	60
High school	45	55
College	58	42
Under $5,000	41	59
$5,000–$9,999	49	51
$10,000–$14,999	50	50
$15,000 and over	54	46
Black	30	70
White	51	49
Republican	52	48
Democrat	48	52
Independent	49	51

TABLE 7

RATING OF YOUR GOVERNOR ON BEING PRESIDENT

	Total %	East %	Midwest %	South %	West %
Excellent	4	3	2	4	7
Pretty good	17	17	18	16	15
Only fair	28	30	28	27	26
Poor	32	35	29	30	41
Not sure	19	15	23	23	11
Total positive	21	20	20	20	22
Total negative	60	65	57	57	67

TABLE 8

In General, Do You Feel Being a Governor Is Better Experience for Being President or Is Being a Senator Better Experience for Being President?

	Total %	East %	Midwest %	South %	West %
Being Senator	55	47	60	53	62
Being Governor	34	40	30	36	29
Not sure	11	13	10	11	9

TABLE 9

Why Do You Think a U.S. Senator/Governor Would Be Better Experience for the Presidency?

	Total %

U.S. Senator

More understanding, exposure to inner workings of federal, national government	28
Understands national issues, problems better	13
Experience with more than one state—sees country as a whole	10
Knows and had experience with Senate	9
Close to and works with the president	7
More involved in major problems, more knowledgeable and responsible in dealing with them	7
More experience in government	5
Closer to the people	5
Understands foreign and international issues and problems better	4
All other reasons	3

Governor

Governor runs a whole state—like running national government on smaller scale	20
Has experience as an executive—makes decisions, leads the people	15
More contact with the people, knows their needs better	8
More experience	3
Deals with bigger variety of problems, more things	3
Knows more about government and politics	3
Knows local problems better	2

TABLE 9 (*continued*)

	Total %
Senators just make laws, vote—not involved in executive duties	1
All other reasons	2
Don't know	2

TABLE 10

REASONS FOR RATING OF YOUR GOVERNOR ON BEING PRESIDENT

	Total %
"Positive" Reasons	
He's doing a good job, knows how to get things done; qualified, he's a good governor	16
Interested, works for the people, knows what's best for them, dedicated to their needs	7
He's honest, fair, man of conviction; stands up for his beliefs, down to earth	6
Has leadership qualities	1
All other "positive" reasons	2
"Negative" Reasons	
No leadership qualities—e.g., no knowledge, not experienced, not aggressive, poor personality	18
Ineffectual, bad job of running state	16
Don't like, have no confidence in him	6
No interest, concern for people of his state; cut back important programs, hasn't kept promises	6
Just don't think he'd be good president	4
Don't like his policies—differ with mine	3
Keeps raising my taxes, we are overtaxed	3
Too politically influenced, plays too much politics	2
He's dishonest, corrupt	2
Too many outside interests	1
All other "negative" reasons	7
Other Reasons	
He's only been governor a short time, too soon to tell, have to wait and see	7
All other reasons	2
Don't know	15

TABLE 11

OVER THE NEXT 10 YEARS, WHICH ONE LEVEL
OF GOVERNMENT DO YOU THINK WILL PLAY THE
MOST IMPORTANT ROLE IN MAKING DECISIONS
WHICH EFFECT YOU PERSONALLY?

	Federal %	State %	Local %	Not Sure %
Total	52	19	19	10
East	53	19	18	10
Midwest	53	18	20	9
South	51	19	18.	12
West	53	21	19	7
18–29	50	22	21	7
30–49	51	17	22	10
50 and over	56	19	14	11
8th grade	48	20	16	16
High school	51	19	20	10
College	58	19	18	5
Under $5,000	45	18	21	16
$5,000–$9,999	56	19	16	9
$10,000–$14,999	53	20	20	7
$15,000 and over	56	21	19	4
Black	39	17	26	18
White	54	19	18	9

TABLE 12

IMPORTANCE OF GOVERNMENT AT ALL LEVELS IN PERSONAL LIVES

	Federal %	State %	Local %
Very important	64	48	46
Somewhat important	21	35	26
Slightly important	7	10	17
Not important at all	2	2	5
Not sure	6	5	6

TABLE 13

The Importance of the Government's Role in Making Decisions Which Affect You Personally Now

	Total %	East %	Mid-west %	South %	West %	18–29 %	30–49 %	50 and Over %	8th Grade %	High School %	College %	Under $5,000 %	$5,000–$9,999 %	$10,000–$14,999 %	$15,000 and Over %	Black %	White %
State Government																	
Very important	48	45	50	47	48	47	48	47	40	49	50	41	48	52	49	37	50
Somewhat important	35	39	34	30	37	38	37	30	30	35	38	29	35	35	41	26	35
Slightly important	10	10	10	11	8	11	8	11	16	9	8	15	9	8	8	20	9
Not important at all	2	2	2	3	4	2	1	4	3	2	2	6	1	1	2	6	2
Not sure	5	4	4	9	3	2	6	8	11	5	2	9	7	4	*	11	4
Local Government																	
Very important	46																
Somewhat important	26																
Slightly important	17																
Not important at all	5																
Not sure	6																
Federal Government																	
Very important	64																
Somewhat important	21																
Slightly important	7																
Not important at all	2																
Not sure	6																

TABLE 14

WHAT DO YOU THINK ARE THE 2 OR 3 MOST VALUABLE SERVICES
YOUR STATE GOVERNMENT PERFORMS FOR ITS RESIDENTS (Voluntary)

	Total %
Education	38
Highways	35
Public health services	16
Police protection, law enforcement, state police	16
Welfare	12
Provides parks, recreation areas	10
Pollution control	5
Aid to aged	3
Housing	3
Higher education—state supported universities	3
Other transportation	3
Mental health facilities	2
Unemployment insurance	2
Employment and Manpower programs	2
Help farmers	1
Making and updating state laws, codes, etc.	1
Collect taxes	1
Other natural resources	1
Motor vehicle control	*
Runs jails	*
Regulates business	*
All other services	11
Doesn't do anything for us	7
Don't know	19

TABLE 15

WHERE KEY POLICY DECISIONS SHOULD BE MADE

	State %	*Local* %	*Federal* %	*Not Sure* %
Education	51	21	23	5
Transportation	41	21	29	9
Prison reform	38	5	50	7
Welfare	36	20	39	5
Housing	36	29	28	7
Health insurance	29	11	49	11
Drug reform	23	16	55	6
Pollution control	20	16	58	6
Cancer research	10	5	77	8
Social	10	2	85	3
National defense	3	1	92	4

TABLE 16

WHERE STATE SHOULD SPEND "LARGEST AMOUNT" OF FEDERAL REVENUE SHARING DOLLARS

	Aid to Education %	Health %	Programs for the Poor %	Pollution Control %	Low and Moderate Income Housing %	Mass Transportation %	Highways %
Total	37	25	15	10	6	4	3
East	34	26	16	8	9	4	3
Midwest	40	23	15	10	5	4	3
South	40	29	15	6	2	3	5
West	31	18	12	20	7	9	3
18–29	42	21	13	13	6	3	2
30–49	40	20	15	10	6	5	4
50 and over	30	32	15	8	5	6	4
8th grade	31	32	19	5	7	1	5
High school	35	27	17	10	5	3	3
College	45	17	9	12	6	8	3
Under $5,000	25	34	21	6	7	4	3
$5,000–$9,999	39	23	15	11	4	3	5
$10,000–$14,999	43	19	14	11	6	5	2
$15,000 and over	40	23	9	14	4	7	3
Black	38	21	27	2	8	2	2
White	36	25	13	12	5	5	4

TABLE 17

IF YOU HAD TO CHOOSE, WOULD YOU PREFER TO SEE
THE NEW MONEY FROM FEDERAL REVENUE SHARING USED
TO IMPROVE AND EXPAND NEEDED PROGRAMS IN THE STATE,
OR USED TO REPLACE CURRENT MONEY BEING SPENT
ON PROGRAMS SO TAXES COULD BE LOWERED?

	Improve and Expand Needed Programs %	*Lower Taxes* %	*Not Sure* %
Total	40	47	13
East	39	48	13
Midwest	39	51	10
South	42	43	15
West	38	47	15
18–29	47	40	13
30–49	38	49	13
50 and over	35	51	14
8th grade	32	49	19
High school	37	49	14
College	48	42	10
Under $5,000	35	47	18
$5,000–$9,999	39	48	13
$10,000–$14,999	41	49	10
$15,000 and over	47	41	12
Black	57	29	14
White	38	50	12

TABLE 18

WHICH ONE FORM OF TAX, REGARDLESS OF HOW IT AFFECTS YOU PERSONALLY, DO YOU FEEL IS THE FAIREST WAY TO RAISE FUNDS?

	Total %	East %	Mid-west %	South %	West %	18–29 %	30–49 %	50 and Over %	8th Grade %	High School %	College %	Under $5,000 %	$5,000–$9,999 %	$10,000–$14,999 %	$15,000 and Over %
State Tax															
Property tax	9	9	10	10	7	12	8	8	8	10	9	6	11	10	9
Sales tax	46	38	39	57	52	46	45	47	44	46	45	48	46	45	43
Income tax	32	39	39	17	33	30	37	30	25	30	40	24	30	35	43
Other	1	1	2	1	1	1	2	1	1	2	1	1	2	1	1
Not sure	12	13	10	15	7	11	8	14	22	12	5	21	11	9	4
Local Tax															
Property tax	24														
Sales tax	40														
Income tax	22														
Other	1														
Not sure	13														
Federal Tax															
Property tax	7														
Sales tax	28														
Income tax	53														
Other	1														
Not sure	11														

TABLE 19

WHICH ONE TAX DO YOU FEEL IS THE BEST FOR YOU—
THE ONE THAT COSTS YOU THE LEAST MONEY?

	Sales Tax %	Property Tax %	Income Tax %	Other %	Not Sure %
Total	35	26	24	1	14
East	34	25	26	1	14
Midwest	37	28	24	1	10
South	30	25	21	2	22
West	41	26	24	1	8
Cities	29	37	24	1	9
Suburbs	41	20	26	1	12
Towns	33	27	23	2	15
Rural	39	18	21	2	20
18–29	27	39	21	*	13
30–49	44	23	20	1	12
50 and over	33	20	28	2	17
8th grade	31	21	24	2	22
High school	35	24	25	1	15
College	38	32	21	1	8
Under $5,000	27	23	28	1	21
$5,000–$9,999	31	29	25	1	14
$10,000–$14,999	41	28	19	1	11
$15,000 and over	43	25	21	2	9
Black	20	38	16	1	25
White	37	25	24	1	13

TABLE 20

How Serious a Problem Do You Think Corruption Is in Government?

	Total %	East %	Mid-west %	South %	West %	18–29 %	30–49 %	50 and Over %	8th Grade %	High School %	College %	Under $5,000 %	$5,000–$9,999 %	$10,000–$14,999 %	$15,000 and Over %
State Government															
Very serious	38	45	31	41	28	35	33	42	40	38	35	40	38	35	35
Somewhat serious	36	33	44	31	38	41	39	30	25	36	41	27	39	39	38
Not really serious	18	17	16	20	22	16	20	19	18	19	18	21	15	19	21
Not sure	8	5	9	8	12	8	8	9	17	7	6	12	8	7	6
Local Government															
Very serious	31														
Somewhat serious	29														
Not really serious	32														
Not sure	8														
Federal Government															
Very serious	52														
Somewhat serious	29														
Not really serious	11														
Not sure	8														

TABLE 21

THE ONE LEVEL WHERE CORRUPTION
HAS HAD THE GREATEST IMPACT

	Total %
Federal level	54
State level	17
Local level	14
Not sure	15

TABLE 22

INFLUENCE OF KEY ELEMENTS ON FEDERAL,
STATE, AND LOCAL GOVERNMENT

	State %	Local %	Federal %
Great Deal of Influence			
Large corporations	63	48	69
Banks and financial institutions	56	52	59
Organized labor	48	35	58
Electric and gas utilities	47	41	41
Organized crime	27	23	31
Farmers	24	23	20
Environmentalists	14	15	15
Ralph Nader	11	7	24
The average citizen	8	19	7
Women's rights groups	5	8	7

TABLE 23

INFLUENCE OF KEY GROUPS ON STATE DECISIONS

	Total %	East %	Mid-west %	South %	West %	Cit-ies %	Sub-urbs %	Towns %	Rural %	18-29 %	30-49 %	50 and Over %	8th Grade %	High School %	Col-lege %	Under $5,000 %	$5,000-$9,999 %	$10,000-$14,999 %	$15,000 and Over %
Large Corporations																			
Great deal	63	67	60	58	68	63	69	59	59	63	65	60	51	62	69	59	58	66	71
Only some	24	23	27	23	24	29	21	24	22	27	22	24	18	26	25	18	27	26	25
Hardly any	4	3	5	5	3	3	4	5	4	3	5	4	5	4	3	5	5	3	2
Not sure	9	7	8	14	5	5	6	12	15	7	8	12	26	8	3	18	10	5	2
Banks and Financial Institutions																			
Great deal	56	66	51	51	57	58	62	52	49	53	58	55	46	58	58	53	52	58	63
Only some	28	24	32	28	30	31	25	31	27	34	27	25	21	28	32	22	31	31	29
Hardly any	6	2	7	7	6	5	6	5	8	6	5	7	7	5	6	6	6	5	5
Not sure	10	8	10	14	7	6	7	12	16	7	10	13	26	9	4	19	11	6	3
Organized Labor																			
Great deal	48	53	53	42	53	56	52	43	43	48	52	48	35	50	56	44	46	50	58
Only some	33	35	29	33	33	33	33	32	31	36	31	31	30	32	34	28	34	35	35
Hardly any	9	5	9	11	8	6	8	14	9	9	8	9	11	9	6	10	10	8	5
Not sure	10	7	9	14	6	5	7	11	17	7	9	12	24	9	4	18	10	7	2

Electric & Gas Utilities

Great deal	46	52	42	43	53	48	51	44	45	45	52	46	41	47	50	43	43	47	57
Only some	36	35	38	35	34	39	35	36	32	41	33	34	29	37	37	30	37	42	33
Hardly any	7	4	10	7	4	6	6	6	6	5	6	7	4	7	7	8	8	5	6
Not sure	11	9	10	15	9	7	8	14	17	9	9	13	26	9	6	20	12	6	4

Organized Crime

Great deal	27	34	20	27	24	29	28	24	23	28	26	26	26	29	24	29	25	27	25
Only some	34	40	36	30	30	37	37	33	30	38	35	32	22	34	40	25	36	39	35
Hardly any	24	15	28	25	32	25	22	25	25	22	23	26	23	23	26	22	25	23	29
Not sure	15	11	16	18	14	9	13	18	22	12	16	16	29	14	10	24	14	11	11

Farmers

Great deal	24	29	24	16	26	25	26	20	21	26	25	21	16	23	28	18	21	24	31
Only some	41	39	43	41	45	45	47	38	37	44	44	38	32	41	48	36	39	47	47
Hardly any	25	22	25	29	23	23	19	33	27	21	23	30	27	27	20	25	29	23	21
Not sure	10	10	8	14	6	7	8	9	15	9	8	11	25	9	4	21	11	6	1

Environmentalists

Great deal	14	15	13	12	19	17	14	15	12	16	17	11	8	14	18	11	13	17	17
Only some	42	49	44	32	46	47	46	38	33	47	43	37	23	44	47	27	42	48	50
Hardly any	28	25	28	31	26	26	29	29	29	27	26	31	29	27	30	28	29	27	29
Not sure	16	11	15	25	9	10	11	18	26	10	14	21	40	15	5	34	16	8	4

Ralph Nader

Great deal	11	14	11	7	12	12	10	11	10	10	11	11	11	12	8	11	11	9	11
Only some	30	33	33	24	27	32	31	30	25	32	32	26	15	30	35	23	29	36	32
Hardly any	41	38	39	44	50	43	45	42	37	43	41	41	30	40	51	35	39	44	50
Not sure	18	15	17	25	11	13	14	17	28	15	16	22	44	18	6	31	21	11	7

234 Many Sovereign States

TABLE 23 (continued)

INFLUENCE OF KEY GROUPS ON STATE DECISIONS

	Total %	East %	Mid-west %	South %	West %	Cit-ies %	Sub-urbs %	Towns %	Rural %	18-29 %	30-49 %	50 and Over %	8th Grade %	High School %	Col-lege %	Under $5,000 %	$5,000-$9,999 %	$10,000-$14,999 %	$15,000 and Over %
The Average Citizen																			
Great deal	8	11	7	8	7	8	5	9	11	10	8	7	9	8	8	8	9	7	8
Only some	35	33	35	38	32	32	34	38	37	39	34	32	25	35	40	26	33	42	39
Hardly any	49	49	51	42	54	56	55	43	39	45	51	51	45	50	49	49	49	47	52
Not sure	8	7	7	12	5	4	6	10	13	6	7	10	21	7	3	17	9	4	1
Women's Rights Groups																			
Great deal	5	7	5	6	3	6	4	9	4	5	5	6	8	6	3	6	6	5	3
Only some	29	34	30	22	31	33	31	22	25	35	27	26	21	29	32	23	30	31	32
Hardly any	54	49	51	57	58	51	56	57	53	52	56	53	41	53	61	48	51	57	61
Not sure	12	10	14	15	8	10	9	12	18	8	12	15	30	12	4	23	13	7	4

TABLE 24

Looking Ahead over the Next 10 Years or So, What Will Be the Importance of Government's Role in Making Decisions Which Affect You Personally Compared to Now?

	Total %	East %	Mid-west %	South %	West %	18-29 %	30-49 %	50 and Over %	8th Grade %	High School %	College %	Under $5,000 %	$5,000-$9,999 %	$10,000-$14,999 %	$15,000 and Over %	Black %	White %
State Government																	
More important role	37	37	36	37	40	41	39	33	29	35	46	32	37	37	43	33	38
Less important role	11	9	12	12	13	13	10	11	10	10	14	10	11	11	15	7	12
About the same	44	47	45	40	39	41	43	45	44	47	36	45	44	44	39	49	42
Not sure	8	7	7	11	8	5	8	11	17	8	4	13	8	8	3	11	8
Local Government																	
More important role	36																
Less important role	11																
About the same	44																
Not sure	9																
Federal Government																	
More important role	46																
Less important role	10																
About the same	35																
Not sure	9																

TABLE 25

INVOLVEMENT OF BUSINESS IN HELPING TO SOLVE GOVERNMENT PROBLEMS IN THE FUTURE

	Total %	East %	Mid-west %	South %	West %	8th Grade %	High School %	College %	Under $5,000 %	$5,000–$9,999 %	$10,000–$14,999 %	$15,000 and Over %	Profes-sional, Executive %	Clerical, Sales %	Skilled %
State Level															
Business should be more involved	50	50	51	44	57	41	48	57	43	48	49	62	56	51	47
Not an area for business involvement	36	37	36	36	33	31	37	36	35	39	38	31	36	36	35
Not sure	14	13	13	20	10	28	15	7	22	13	13	7	8	13	18
Local Level															
Business should be more involved	61														
Not an area for business involvement	27														
Not sure	12														
Federal Level															
Business should be more involved	42														
Not an area for business involvement	43														
Not sure	15														

TABLE 26

KNOWLEDGE OF YOUR GOVERNOR'S POLITICAL PARTY

	Know Correctly %	Don't Know %
Total	*81*	*19*
East	79	21
Midwest	85	15
South	75	25
West	86	14
18–29	72	28
30–49	83	17
50 and over	86	14
8th grade	69	31
High school	79	21
College	90	10
Under $5,000	75	25
$5,000–$9,999	77	23
$10,000–$14,999	84	16
$15,000 and over	88	12
Black	55	45
White	84	16
Republican	87	13
Democrat	80 .	20
Independent	78	22

Notes

1. Sharkansky, Ira, *The Maligned States*, McGraw-Hill Book Co., New York, 1972, p. 2.
2. Sanford, Terry, *Storm Over the States*, McGraw-Hill Book Co., New York, 1967, p. 21.
3. Grodzins, Morton, "The Federal System," *Goals for Americans, Report of the President's Commission on National Goals*, Prentice-Hall, Inc., New Jersey.
4. Sanford, *op. cit.*, p. 31.
5. Brandeis, Louis D., *New York State Ice Co. v. Libman*, 205 US 262, (1932).
6. Patterson, James T., *The New Deal and the States, Federalism in Transition*, Princeton, Princeton University Press, 1969, p. 7.
7. Patterson, *op. cit.*, p. 10.
8. Allen, Robert S., *Our Sovereign States*, New York, The Vanguard Press, Inc., 1949, VII.
9. Allen, *op. cit.*, XII.
10. Burns, John, *The Sometime Governments*, Bantam Books, New York City, 1971, p. 3.
11. Patterson, *op. cit.*, p. 61.
12. Burns, *op. cit.*, p. 16.
13. Grad, Frank P., *The State's Capacity to Respond to Urban Problems: The State Constitution*, Campbell, *op. cit.*, p. 29.
14. Grad, *op. cit.*, p. 29.
15. Sanford, *op. cit.*, p. 29.
16. Grad, *op. cit.*, p. 30.
17. Allen, *op. cit.*, XXXI.
18. Broder, David S., *The Party's Over*, Harper & Row, New York, 1971, p. 157.

19. Peirce, Neal R., *The Megastates of America*, W. W. Norton & Company, Inc., New York, 1972, p. 595.

20. The Council of State Government, *The Book of States: 1974–1975*, published by the Council of State Government, Box 11910, Lexington, Kentucky, 40511.

21. Neuberger, Richard, *Adventures in Politics*, Oxford University Press, New York, 1954, p. 5.

22. Rogers, John C., "LEAP—How to Save $75 Million," *Parade*, March 4, 1973.

23. *Ibid.*

24. Mintz, Morton, and Cohen, Jerry S., *America, Inc.*, Dell Publishing Co., Inc., New York, 1971, p. 9.

25. *Support Your City—Support Revenue Sharing*—a publication of the US Conference of Mayors, Washington, D.C., 1973, p. 2.

26. Gaffney, Mason, "In Praise of the Property Tax," *The Washington Monthly*, February 1973, p. 3.

27. Advisory Commission on Intergovernmental Relations, Information Bulletin, Number 73-2, Washington D.C., February 1973, p. 2.

28. Bahl, Roy W., *State Taxes, Expenditures and the Fiscal Plight of the Cities*, Campbell, *op. cit.*, p. 104.

29. Nixon, Richard, Revenue Sharing Message to Congress, August 13, 1969.

30. "HEW Department's Categorical-Grant Structure Isolates Governors, Strengthens Bureaucracies," *National Journal*, March 3, 1973, p. 308.

31. Elazar, Daniel J., "The Dilemmas of Revenue Sharing," *Ripon Forum* May, 1972, p. 25.

32. Sharkansky, Ira, *op. cit.*, p. 128.

33. *Ibid.*, p. 37.

34. Sanford, *op. cit.*, p. 111.

35. Trippett, Frank, *The States: United They Fell*, The World Publishing Company, Cleveland, Ohio, 1967, p. 2.

36. Halpern, Paul J., "Organizing for Political Change," *Governing Urban America in the 1970's*, edited by Werner Z. Hirsch and Sidney Sonnerblum, Praeger, New York, 1973, p. 181.

37. Sanford, *op. cit.*, p. 67.

38. Trippett, *op. cit.*, p. 208.
39. Elazar, Daniel J., "The States and the Nation," *Politics in the American States*, edited by Hubert Jacobs and Kenneth N. Vines, Boston, Little, Brown & Co., 1965, p. 449.
40. White, Theodore, *The Making of the President—1972*, p. 206.
41. Broder, *op. cit.*, p. 264.
42. Frankel, Max, "Revenue Sharing Is a Counter-Revolution," *New York Times Magazine*, as quoted by Broder, *op. cit.*, p. 151.

INDEX

Adams, Samuel, 22
Advisory Commission on Intergovernmental Relations (ACIR), 109
air pollution. *See* Clean-air programs
Airport and Airways Development Act, 176
Allen, Robert S. *(Our Sovereign States)*, 30, 46, 192
Anderson, Wendell, 87
Articles of Confederation, 21, 22, 24, 26, 41, 185
"Articles of Perpetual Union," 21
Ashley, Thomas L., 207
Askew, governor of Florida, 65

"Bacillus Thuringiensis [B.T.] Caper," 152–53
Bahl, Roy W., 111
Bailey, John, 57
Baldrige, Malcolm, 82
Bampton, Ted, 195, 198

Beck, Chris, 38, 211
Beverage Container Act, 161
bond issues as source of local revenue, 105
Book of the States, 45
Bowlby, Rita, 6
Brandeis, Louis D., 27, 28
Brenneman, Russ, 10
Breslin, Jimmy, 44
British North America Act, 23
Broder, David *(The Party's Over)*, 46, 209
Bueche, Arthur, 82
bureaucracy: in federal government, 13, 75, 121, 123–24, 129–37, 166; in state government, 8–9, 26–27, 38–39, 71–75, 80–81, 101–3, 107, 117, 129–30
business and industry: in government–industrial combines, 92–93; government regulation of, 76–77, 85–86, 90; as political pressure groups, 46–47, 58–59, 193;